GLOBAL TRENDS IN HUMAN RIGHTS EDUCATION

Sarat C. Joshi

FORWARD BOOKS
NEW DELHI • GUWAHATI • VISAKHAPATNAM

FORWARD BOOKS
4649-B/21, Ansari Road
Darya Ganj, New Delhi - 110 002
Ph.: 23263193 / 9811582579 / 09435116718
Fax: 011-23263193
Email: ektabooks@yahoo.com
www.akanshapublishinghouse.com

Global Trends in Human Rights Education

First Published 2011

ISBN 978-81-909742-4-0

PRINTED IN INDIA

Published by Forward Books, New Delhi and Printed at S.N. Printers, Delhi.

PREFACE

> "All human beings are born free and equal in dignity and rights. They are endowed with reason and sonscience and should act towards one another in a spirit of brotherhood [and sisterhood]."
>
> —*UDHR, Article I*

Human Rights Education is a deliberate, participatory practice aimed at empowering individuals, groups and communities through fostering knowledge, skills and attitudes consistent with internationally recognized human rights principles. All governments have a duty to teach regularly about human rights and to provide a learning experience and environment where human rights are respected and acknowledged.

Coming to human rights education, no formal system was there in yore days. But respect for others, dignify all persons, treating all equal and other such habits were cultivated in infants and children in every household. Moral values and ethics were given emphasis.

The U.N. Special Rapporteur on the Right to Education has expressed the view that human rights education is an integral part to the right to education. Integration of human rights into the education system contributes to ensuring the construction of quality education and to improving standards of living for all.

Promotion of rights based approach enables the education system to ensure full development of the human personality, sense of dignity and strength and respect for human rights and fundamental freedoms.

about human rights and to provide a learning experience and environment where human rights are respected and acknowledged.

Amnesty International's newly endorsed international strategy for human rights education embraces this definition and sets the framework for Human Rights Educations until 2010 and aims to:

- Use education to build a global culture of human rights and prevent human rights abuses.
- Enable a broad spectrum of individuals, groups and communities to understand and express their personal concerns in human rights terms.
- Inspire people to integrate human rights principles into both their individual lives and their social institutions.
- Enable people to demand support and defend human rights and use them as a tool for social change.

Four major principles that need to be considered for the implementation of Human Rights Education are:

- It is a long-term planning programmes
- Aids the strategic planning programmes
- Makes use of participatory methods
- Strengthens capacity for effective delivery of Human Rights Education.

United Nations World Programme for Human Rights Education (2005-)

The United Nations's World Programme of Human Rights Education and Plan of Action proposes a comprehensive implementation strategy for the national level. The main responsibility for implementation rests with the Ministry of Education in each country. Member states are encouraged to identify and support a resource center for collecting and disseminating initiatives and information on human rights education (good practices from diverse contexts and countries).

OHCHR and UNESCO are taking steps to disseminate the Plan of Action and will assist states to implement it.

The U.N. Special Rapporteur on the Right to Education has expressed the view that human rights education is an integral part to the right to education. Integration of human rights into the education system contributes to ensuring the construction of quality education and to improving standards of living for all.

Promotion of rights based approach enables the education system to ensure full development of the human personality, sense of dignity and strength and respect for human rights and fundamental freedoms.

There is need to recognize education as a human rights rather than an economic good and member states have an obligation to implement this right. The human rights dimension of education needed to be strengthened with out looking at education from an utilitarian perspective that guarantees an economic result. A lot of people see education as a service, business and a way to improve the economic struggle against poverty.

This view is not in dispute, but the aim of education is linked to human dignity and to the realization of human rights of individuals that member states have an obligation to implement. The main obstacle to progress on the right to education is that it has been "de-linked" from a culture of respect for human rights. In order to over come this obstacle human rights learning and education are mechanisms that could allow us to transform patriarchal practices that reduce education to a mechanism that perpetuates existing social and cultural traditions and practices, regardless of their impact on human rights.

The other areas identified as obstacles to the enjoyment of the right to education are tuition fees, lack of teachers and poverty combined with inferior position given to education in national budgets. Primary education is the foundation of the whole system. If we can improve access to it, we can avoid drop outs at primary level and ensure continuation to secondary level. As for example, abolition of tuition fees saw an increase in school attendance in Kenya, Malawi, Tanzania and Uganda, reason being that education is regarded more as a cost than an investment in developing countries.

The first sentence of the preamble of the Universal Declaration of Human Rights states that recognition and respect for human rights is the "foundation of freedom, peace and justice in the world". Indeed, the denial of human rights is not only an individual or personal tragedy, but also creates conditions of social unrest and political turmoil and sows seeds of conflict between societies and nations. However, for proper implementation of human rights it is necessary for everyone to know about his or her own rights, There is always a close relationship between legislation, implementation and education.

Indeed, know your rights is the message of the United Nations. Article 26(2) of the Universal Declaration of Human Rights says that "education shall be directed for the full development of the human personality" and to the strengthening of respect for human rights and fundamental freedom. This message is important because only the people who are aware of their rights can ensure that their rights will not be trampled on. Learning about one's own rights builds respect for the rights of others and gives confidence to assert them. The general conference of the United Nations Educational, Scientific and Cultural Organization (UNESCO) at its eighteenth session in Paris in 1974 recommended that "education should be directed for the full development of the human personality and to the strengthening of respect for human rights and fundamental freedom.

It shall promote understanding, tolerance and friendship among all nations, racial or religious groups, and shall further the activities of the United Nations for the sake of peace". The document, further stated that education should stress the inadmissibility of recourse to war for the purpose of aggression or domination or use of force or violence for purpose of repression and bring every person to understand or assume his or her responsibilities for the maintenance of peace.

Teheran Conference

Earlier at the International Conference on Human Rights (1968) held in Teheran it was decided to call on States to ensure that all "means of education should be used to stimulate interest in the problems of human right in the changing world". The United Nations General Assembly resolved in the same year to take steps, according to the scholastic system of each State, to introduce and encourage principles proclaimed in the Universal Declaration of Human Rights and other Declarations. It urged on the teachers to draw attention of the students on every possible occasion to this growing role of the United Nations in fostering co-operative efforts for the promotion of social justice and human rights throughout the world. Indeed UNESCO has played a very prominent role in the promotion of human rights education.

The International Congress on the Teaching of Human Rights (Vienna, 1978), UNESCO International Congress on Human Rights Teaching, Information and Documentation (Malta, 1987) dealt with principles and considerations that should guide the teaching of human rights. Recommendations of these two conferences unequivocally mentioned that human rights teaching and education must aim at fostering an attitude of tolerance, respect and solidarity inherent in human rights, provide knowledge of human rights in both national and international dimensions and develop among the individuals awareness of the ways/and means by which human rights can be translated into social and political reality at both national and international levels. Education should not only make the individual aware of his or her own rights but should also at the same time instill respect for the rights of others.

Plan of Action

The World Plan of Action adopted by the International Congress for Education and Democracy in Montreal (March, 1993) calls for global mobilisation of the resources from the family to the United Nations to educate individuals and groups about human rights so that inappropriate conduct leading to a denial of human rights will be changed. Learning is not an end in itself, but rather the means of ending violations of human rights and building a culture of peace based on democracy, development, tolerance and human respect.

The document "Plan of Action" by UNESCO further mentions that though the cold war has come to an end and walls have come down, the last decade of the twentieth century is witnessing the recurrence of most serious human rights violations caused by racism, xenophobia, sexism and religious intolerance. No less disturbing for the protection of human fights are the threats stemming from environmental degradation, from new biomedical technologies and from the scourge of HIV/AIDS.

Against this sombre background one has to think and work out proper strategies for education of human rights. It is true that education cannot eliminate the conditions that cause massive violation of human rights and even affect human survival. There are various social, political and economic factors responsible for this. But education does indeed liberate the mind of the individual and provide him the capacity and motivation to act. Human rights implies universality. Education in human rights should make an individual conscious of the basic and-inalienable rights of others, regardless of sex, language, religion and other social and economic conditions. It will enable them to become more responsible citizens not only of their own countries but of the world.

Vienna Conference

Therefore, in today's changing world education for human rights is an imperative need-education that will liberate minds from the thraldom of obscurantism, bigotry and narrowness and nurture democratic values and promote a societal transformation based on human rights culture. This explains why the World Conference on Human Rights held at Vienna in 1993 reaffirmed that States are duty-bound, as stipulated in the Universal Declaration of Human Rights and the International Covenant on Economic, Social and Cultural Rights and in other international human rights instruments, to ensure that education promotes respect for human rights and fundamental freedom. States must work out education programmes that promote tolerance and foster peace and understanding among the nations as well as different social, religious and ethnic groups. There is an ongoing debate among the educationists and human rights activists about the manner of teaching human rights in schools and colleges. Some experts are of the view that human rights should be a study subject in the same way as mathematics, science and history and only in this way human rights topics can acquire due status in the curriculum.

Other school is of the opinion that human rights contents should be included in every subject and thus it will pervade all school and college tasks. In the words of Jose Ayala Lasso, the former United Nations High Commissioner for Human Rights "the objective of all human rights educational activity should be to teach the common language of humanity. Human rights should not be one subject of education, but should permeate all aspects of education in all forms".

Sikri Committee on HRE

In India way back in 1980, the University Grants Commission set up a Committee under Mr. Justice S.M. Sikri to consider different ways and means for promoting human rights education in India. The Committee suggested different approaches at different levels of education. At schools and +2 levels human rights values could be best inculcated through stories, poems, biographies and similar other literature. School children should not be over-burdened with human rights teaching for the purpose of securing marks at the examinations.

Emphasis should be on inculcating human rights values on their impressionable minds. For achieving this, human rights teaching should not remain confined to the open curriculum of the school. They must also find reflection in the 'hidden curriculum', in the creation of a school atmosphere that displays respect for human rights. An important aim of human rights education for children at the elementary school stage should be to develop in their impressionable minds positive attitudes and values. This can be ensured by providing a democratic environment, enabling children to enjoy their rights and simultaneously learn to respect the rights of others. In our country it is very important to expose children at the early school stage to the concept of one world and Human Rights because many children for a variety of reasons do not go beyond the elementary level of schooling. A child at this stage is normally very energetic, curious as well as socially and morally conscious.

Development of broader outlook and constructive attitudes formed in the middle and later childhood will enable children to grow into responsible and mature citizens with constant concern for human rights of other. At the secondary school level, knowledge is to be presented more systematically and the students should be encouraged to develop some capacity for action. With greater intellectual maturity of the students there is scope for teaching the curriculum subjects in a more imaginative and interactive manner. Resources such as libraries, museums, press, cinema, television etc., should be exploited for conveying correctly the message of human rights. The Sikri Committee was of the clear view that at college and university levels values and concepts of human rights can be taught through books and other lessons. The committee also felt that even graduate students in science, commerce, medicine should be exposed to certain perspectives of human rights, at least such aspects of human rights which are directly relevant to their discipline. At postgraduate level, the concerned departments of Political Science/ Law in- selected universities should introduce a diploma course in human rights.

Adult Education Programmes

Teaching of human rights in adult education programmes

should have a practical orientation. Mere teaching the adults what constitutes human rights is not adequate. Adult education programmes should be utilized to stress among the adults, the need to defend human rights and fight against abuse of authority. In that context the practical value of adults organizing themselves in associations or groups should also be emphasized. Adult education programmes should also harp on the message that•violations of human rights are frequent and rampant because the people are not active and vigilant. Denial of human rights even to one person should be a matter of concern for the entire community Indeed, eternal vigilance is the price of liberty Unfortunately/it is seen that text books vary from State to State. Contents in many text books negate the basic concepts of human rights and dignity.

Text books used in schools in many parts of "the country reflect communal, casteist, linguistic distortions and gender bias. There are materials used in some schools which are purposely designed to foster bigotry Efforts at imparting proper human rights education to young and impressionable minds will fail if steps are not taken by the authorities to remove these distortions from the textbooks. The National Human Rights Commission has been informed that the National Council of Educational Research and Training (NCERT) is now conducting a programme of text book evaluation, mainly of history books and in some States of language text books from the viewpoint of national integration. Under this programme caste, linguistic and gender biases and distortions noticed in the text books are identified and state educational authorities are advised to take steps to remove them. NCERT proposes to extend the scope of evaluation to other issues which are more directly specific to human rights. In devising teaching methodology, it has to be kept in mind that an educational course is effective if it is rooted in the concrete situations faced by the students.

Every curriculum should take into account real-life issues and problems of the students concerned and examine them and suggest appropriate ways of dealing with them. Students should be encouraged to ponder over these issues and come out with their suggestions. This interactive or participatory mode of learning should become a part of the actual classroom pedagogy. Mere formal and theoretical instruction will not help in the sensitization of the students. For this purpose, co-curricular and extracurricular programmes like staging of plays and debates, essay competitions, seminars reflecting human rights problems have to be promoted. This will not only foster an awareness of human rights among the students, but will also motivate them to play a legitimate interventionist role in certain situations.

In any training or teaching programme, the role of the committed teacher/ trainers is of crucial importance. Teachers are the pivots around which all education revolves. Any attempt to introduce human rights education in schools will not be successful unless teachers educators are properly oriented. In the field of human rights teacher's own perception of human rights and commitments will count more than any well-prepared curriculum and elaborate guidelines. Unfortunately, teacher preparation is another major area of weakness. So far very little has been done to sensitize the teachers on human rights issues. In a paper titled "Education for Human Rights and Democracy in Indian Schools' presented by Dr. A.K. Sharma, Director NCERT, it was mentioned that there have been instances when teachers have expressed their reluctance to make available the text of the Convention on the Rights of the child to the students on the ground that it would create problems of indiscipline. Indeed teachers' attitude, style and responses will strengthen or undermine students commitment to human rights.

In this connection it has to be borne in mind that in the transference process of knowledge about human rights, teaching methods which emphasize a hierarchical and authoritarian relationship between teachers and students has to be discouraged. This kind of transference will be self-defeating and will distort the content of human rights. The manner in which the knowledge of human rights is imparted is interwoven with the essence of human rights content. An interactive approach which allows learners to pause and think over the underlying principles of human rights and imbibe them and reflect them in his work and conduct is needed. The mass communication media can play a very effective role in the advancement of human rights. Radio and television,, if proper and thoughtful programmes are drawn up, can carry the message of human rights in every corner of the country and can shape and mould thinking of the people on human rights issues. They can serve as powerful instruments for advancement of human rights and sensitise the society against suppression and violation of human rights.

Human Rights Education for Social Change

From the day, society started functioning, intention to light and to war with other societies, began in the minds of men. And Joad on Civilization stated that till war is removed from the minds of men, they can never be termed 'Civilized' Development and Advancement of Science at the end of the nineteenth century, predicted, that apart from the promise of comfort and better living conditions. Science can also be used as a negative instrument, for destruction of Human's and devastation of societies. Magnitude of War, increased to such an extent, that warring between two nations was not the order of the day; instead, this destructive feature, engulfed the whole world: it was no longer between nations; it was "World War". Irrespective of whether one belonged to warring nations or not, every human being on earth was affected directly or indirectly by the weapons of global destruction. In the first half of the 20th century, at the close of the World War I, international concern for human rights found expression in certain provisions of the convenant of the League of Nations.

Member States of the League accepted the obligation to endeavour to secure and maintain fair and human conditions of labour for men, women and children and also to ensure the just treatment of the indigenous inhabitants of their colonies. There was a Mandates system established by the Covenant, under which, certain powers accepted as a sacred trust, responsibility for the well-being and development of the peoples, placed under their Mandate. It is to be noted, that at this juncture colonies under the British, as in the case of India, have started their rigorous struggle for political freedom from the yoke of Empire, who was using the Rod of Power, from a distance of ten thousand kilometers and 'meek' Societies were their 'obedient servants'. Declaration of World War II in 1939 put an end to even this apparent concern for the well-being of Colonies-subjects by the Master Powers. But the period of the War, 1939-45, experienced that agony and trauma, hitherto unpredicted by any category of War. With the destruction of two major cities in Japan, (Hiroshima and Nagasaki) and Pearl Harbour in, the West. The Great Powers who were on a "Show-off of their Power of Destruction, had to put an end to the Global Holocast and declare Peace.

The establishment of the UNO, another Global Voluntary Organization, in which the most powerful nations and least-powerful nations, became members from 1945 onwards was the result. Under the several purposes of the United Nations for achievement of international co-operation, promoting and encouraging respect for human rights and for fundamental freedoms for all without distinction as to race, sex, language or religion, was considered indispensable for the survival of humans and their welfare.

This was the consequence of the horrors of World War II and the beastly behaviour of the regimes that unleashed it. Experience of this War, led to the conviction that for ensuring global peace and progress, effective protection of human rights was one of the essential conditions. On 10th December 1948, the General Assembly of the United Nations adopted and proclaimed the Universal Declaration of Human Rights and it stated "as a common standard of achievement for all peoples and all nations, to the end, that every individual and every organ of society, keeping this Declaration constantly in mind, shall store by teaching and Education to promote respect for these rights and freedoms and by progressive measures, national and international, to secure their universal and effective recognition and observance, both among the people of Member States themselves and among the people of territories under their jurisdiction".

The Declaration consists of a preamble and 30 Articles, under which "the human rights and fundamental freedoms, to which all men and women, everywhere, in the World are entitled, without any discrimination". (Universal Declaration of Human Rights-United Nations, New York, 1948).

Article 26 of the Universal Declaration of Human Rights proclaims that "Every one has the right to education". To achieve this goal, the following principles are laid down:

(1) Education shall be free, at least in the elementary

2

Contemporary Developments in Human Rights Education

> "Arise, awake and learn by approaching the excellent (teachers). The intelligent people describe that path (of knowledge) to be as impassable as a razor's edge, which when sharpened, is difficult to tread on."
>
> — *Katha Upanishad (1.3.14)*

Human Rights Education (HRE) has emerged as an academic discipline by now. Many universities has separate departments for and even some institutions are solely imparting human rights education.

In this chapter we will put light on contemporary developments in human rights education.

Mr. Rene Cassin, Nobel Peace Laureate who was mostly responsible for drafting the Universal Declaration of Human Rights, aptly said, 'The science of Human Rights is defined as a particular branch of the social science the object of which is to study the human relations in the light of human dignity while determining those rights and faculties which are necessary as a whole for the full development of each human being's personality". The all-round development of individual's personality and universal peace and harmony can be promoted through suitable human rights education.

The UNESCO has also felt the "desirability of envisaging the systematic study and development of independent scientific disciplines of human rights, taking into account the principal legal system of the world with a view to facilitating the understanding, apprehension, study and teaching of human rights at university level and subsequently at other educational levels". Hence multi-pronged efforts should be made by all concerned-individuals, government and non-government organisations to realise the objectives visualised in the Declaration of Human Rights.

The World War II seriously brought about not only the awareness, but a kind of sensation in the human destiny and inflicted on the mankind by Nazism and Fascism. The atmosphere of insecurity, oppression, discrimination and unjust socio-economic conditions of man prevailed both at the national and international levels as a result of which mankind was very much in quest of peace, harmony and security in the human life through universal commitments. The Charter of United Nations Human Rights was drafted and accepted in 1948 for ensuring social justice and human rights which are felt as basic requirements of stable international order and lasting peace. Therefore, in the Preamble to the Charter, the fathers of the document insisted ". . . to re-affirm faith in the fundamental human rights in the dignity and worth of human person...".

Later on this reference to human rights was taken as the basis for elaboration and the General Assembly of UN adopted the Universal Declaration of Human Rights on the 10th December 1948. This Declaration in itself although has no legal sanction, in a sense it cannot be enforced by any International Court, its provisions and guidelines for aspirations of the mankind and functioning of the government in accordance with the Declaration. A few objectives of the Declaration laid down in the Preamble are given below:

(a) recognition of the inherent dignity of all human beings;

(b) promotion of equality, freedom, justice and peace;

(c) freedom from fear, tyranny, oppression;

(d) promotion of social progress and better standard of/ life;

(e) saving of the succeeding generations from the scourge of war;

(f) providing common standard of achievement for all peoples and all nations; and

(g) development of friendly relations between nations.

Human Rights Declaration proclaimed in 30 Articles may briefly be stated as follows:

(a) All human beings are born free and equal in dignity and rights;

(b) Every one is entitled to this right without discrimination of race, colour, sex, language, conviction, personal opinion, property, birth or other status;

(c) Every one has the right to life, liberty and security;

(d) Slavery/slave trade shall be prohibited in all forms;

(e) No one shall be subjected to torture or to cruel inhuman or degrading punishment,

(f) All are equal before law;

(g) Everyone has right to effective constitutional remedy;

(h) There shall be no interference with the privacy, family and correspondence of an individual;

(i) Everyone has the right, to freedom of movement and residence within the borders of his country, to leave his country and return to it and own property; and

(j) Everyone has the right to freedom of thought, conviction, religion, opinion and expression and peaceful assembly and forming associations, to take part in the Government of his country, to social security, to work and free choice of employment, to equal pay for equal work, just and favourable remuneration for the work, to rest and leisure, to standard of living, declaration of health and well-being of himself and his family, to education that shall be at least at the elementary level and fundamental stages to participate in the cultural life of the community.

In order to trace the genesis of the human rights education, we can refer to the philosophers, social and political thinkers through ages in different countries of the World. Particularly, the concept of "Vasudhaiba Kutumbakam" and "Nara Narayana" contained the spirit of human rights in Indian civilisation. Both in oriental and Occidental literature we found the concepts of equality, fraternity, peace and harmony. Especially Rousseau, Ruskin, Plato and Socrates in the West and Manu, Vyasdeva, Narada Muni and others in India have enunciated with principles of human rights in one form or another. But always duties overweighted rights in the ancient days. However, the latter got prominence at first in the Magna Carta in Britain in 1215 AD, Petition of Rights in 1628 AD.

Habeas Corpus Act 1628 AD, Bill of Rights in 1689, American Declaration of Independence in 1676 AD and Declaration of Rights of Men in France during 1789 AD and subsequently in the Declaration of Universal Human Rights by UN in 1948. In Teheran, an international Congress of Human Rights was organised in 1968. The UN Convened an international Congress on the teaching of Human Rights which was held at Vienna in 1988. The UN World Conference of Human Rights in Vienna in 1993 drafted a Declaration ultimately inspiring the UN Decade for Human Rights Education 1995-2004. Out of the 100 clauses in the Programme of Action (POA) of Vienna Declaration four are related directly to Education and Training which are as follows:

Art. 78: The World Conference of Human Rights consider human rights education, training and public information essential for the promotion and achievement of stable and harmonious relations among communities for mutual understanding, tolerance and peace.

Art. 79: States should strive to eradicate illiteracy and should direct education towards the full development of the human personality and to the strengthening of respect for human lights and fundamental freedoms.

Art. 80: Human Rights Education should include Peace, Democracy, Development and Social justice, as set forth in the international regional human rights instruments in order to achieve common understanding and awareness with a view to strengthening universal commitments to human rights.

Art. 81: Taking into account the World Plan of Action for human rights and democracy, adopted in 1993 by the International Congress on Education for human rights and democracy of the UNESCO and other human rights instruments, the World

> Conference on human rights recommends that states develop specific programmes and strategies for ensuring the widest human rights education and dissemination of public information taking particular account of the human rights needs of women.

Major theme of the World NGO Conference of Decade of Human Rights Education would introduce a culture specificity to the educational process. This was felt to be an uphill task because teaching human rights as a culture issue was recognised by academic as a weakly defined area.

The conservation and preservation of basic human rights should be left to the individuals and groups who have to priorities their own human rights agenda. Prioritisation needs educational base for the efficient performance, because knowledge and information are the two vital inputs for concerted action in this area of information technology. A culture-oriented education is necessary to teach human rights as a vital element in the new human rights agenda. International Convention on the elimination of all forms of racial discrimination was implemented in 1969. This Convention obliges the state parties to

(a) seek to eliminate racial discrimination and promote understanding among the races;
(b) ensure that all public authorities act accordingly;
(c) abolish any laws or regulations which effectively perpetuate racial discrimination;
(d) condemn all propaganda based on various racial superiority or aimed at promoting racial discrimination and to adopt measures to eradicate all incitements to discrimination;

(e) to guarantee the right to equality before law of everyone without discrimination as to the race, colour or nationality or ethnic origin;

(f) ensure protection and remedies against acts of racial discrimination which violate human rights; and

(g) adopt measures especially in culture and nation with a prejudices.

International Convenants on Civil and Political Rights was implemented in 1976 which seeks to guarantee to all, individuals subject to their jurisdiction the rights recognised in it. These Rights are as follows:

(a) Right to life;

(b) Freedom from torture or cruel inhuman degrading treatment;

(c) Freedom from slavery or servitude;

(d) Right to liberty and security to person and freedom from arbitrary arrest and detention;

(e) Right to a fair trial;

(f) Equality before law;

(g) Protection against arbitrary interference with privacy;

(h) Freedom of movement;

(i) Right to nationality;

(j) Right to marry and to found a family;

(k) Freedom of thought, conscience and religion;

(l) Freedom of association and the Right to join a trade union; and

(m) Right to vote and take part in Government.

International Convenants on Economic, Social and Cultural Rights was adopted in 1966 but implemented in 1976. Rights included are as follows:

(a) Right to work;
(b) Right to a fair wage (including for women equal pay for equal work) and form and join trade unions/ associations;
(c) to adequate standard of living;
(d) to education (with the Progressive introduction of free education);
(e) for children, to freedom from exploitation (in accordance with which the state should set a minimum age for admission to paid employment); and
(f) to participate in the cultural life of the community.

The Convention of the Elimination of All Forms of Discrimination Against Women came into force in 1981 and requires the state parties to seek to eliminate discrimination against women in all fields. The States should take temporary measures for accelerating equality between men and women in the following matters:

(a) Right to vote;
(b) Right to be eligible for election to public offices and to hold public offices at all levels;
(c) Right to participate in the formulation of Government policy and in government organisations concerned with public and political life;
(d) Equality before law;
(e) Equal rights as regards nationality; and
(f) Right to work and equal employment opportunities with men including the equal pay for equal work.

Convention on the Rights of the Child passed earlier came into force in 1990. The State parties undertake to protect the child from all kinds of discrimination and to provide appropriate care. The following rights were ensured by the Convention:

(a) Right to life and to protection from capital punishment;
(b) Right to acquire nationality;
(c) Protection from separation from parents;
(d) Right to leave any country and enter his or her own country;
(e) Right to enter or leave another state for the purpose of family reunification;
(f) Right to protection from being illicitly taken abroad or prevented from returning to his or her own country;
(g) Protection of childs interest in adoption cases;
(h) Freedom of thought, conscience and religion;;
(i) Right of access to health care services with state aiming to reduce infant and child mortality and abolish traditional practices, prejudices to health;
(j) Right to adequate standard of living and social security;
(k) Right to education with states making primary education compulsory and free;
(1) Protection from involving in the illicit production, trafficking and use of narcotics, drugs and psychotropic substances; and
(m) Protection from sexual exploitation and abuse.

From the foregoing analysis it has become obvious that human rights education has gained tremendous importance in all societies of the world.

Now we will turn to discuss an efficient and workable strategy for human rights education in the next chapter.

3

HUMAN RIGHTS EDUCATION STRATEGY

> "When, to one who knows, all beings have verily, become and with his own self, then what delusion and what sorrow can be to him who has seen the oneness?"
>
> —*Isha Upanishad*

Paradoxical though it may be humans are not yet prepared to occupy the world they have shaped for themselves -an observation made by far-sighted educators long back but still valid. With fantastic rapidity of changes all around, education faces ever increasing new demands as new ways of coping with the realities of life become necessary. Also the world today is full of the clash of contending forces: Amidst the striking evidence of birth and life, there is also the alarming incidence of death and destruction. Along with aspirations rising sky-high cherished ideals keep crumbling to the ground. With the spread of money and muscle power, complex forms of exploitation, abuse and deprivation take place adding many more subtle dimensions to the denial of human rights, thus causing untold suffering to human beings. The ground realities in the world around us may be shocking at times, even more so in countries like India with a strong spiritual tradition, known as proverbial land of Gods and goddesses.

Therefore, this accordingly, approaches the crucial area of human rights in the light of an expressed suggestion in UN Charter of Human Rights relevant documents: The formulation of strategies and programmes for FIRE The rationale is developed on the basis of HR-HRE related literature-UN professional organisations and voluntary, peoples organisations, groups. In this matrix the paper reiterates, deals with and or highlights most of the important givens, meaningful major ideas, concerns components. Human Rights as a global value, holistic concept, pivotal role of HRE with special reference to the nature and scope of HR. It considers the inclusion of HRE in educational institutions across the ladder, emphasises HRE as a component of the basic integrated core curriculum at school level. Suggests HRE orientation inputs into professional courses and specialised training programmes for defence and civil services! It goes on to identify selected urgent and, for all practical purposes, prime short-term goals achieving the long term ideal goals, vision; these all for immediate action for a better tomorrow.

In this context the paper stresses simultaneous initiatives for supportive action and activities through parallel alternative channels, reinforced from every available forum and with all new age techniques. While doing so, the implementation and enforcement aspects are also dealt with. The paper concludes with an appeal to educators as champions of HR to act through consensus and with solidarity for fulfilling their commitment to HR-HRE.

UN Decade for HRE : 1995-2005

The proclamation of the UN Decade for Human Rights Education, January 1995 has placed the long-felt need of HRE in much sharper focus today than ever: A landmark in itself, it is a powerful reminder to member states and people across the world of the Human Rights instruments to plan appropriately for future. The UN Decade is indeed a call for multipronged global action at various levels to promote, protect and ensure the inherent dignity of human life everywhere Although the United Nations and related agencies, professional and voluntary organisations have also contributed significantly to the recognition and importance of human rights education WGGI, the World Council for Curriculum & Instruction declared in 1970 in the Preamble to its Constitution. "As members of the World community, educators have a responsibility to ensure that education contributes to the promotion of equity, peace and the universal realisation of human rights".... Human Rights and Values related themes and issues have since received attention especially in India.

The World Confederation of the Organisations of the Teaching Profession, the winner of Nobel Peace Prize and UN Human Rights Peace Prize reiterates its commitment from time to time, to the rights ànd duties of the teaching community and to human rights and values in general.

The People's Decade for Human Rights Education 1991-2001, in action since the late 1980, has organised and promoted Human Rights Education activities in many parts of the world bringing visibility to HRE. In fact, it was involved in preparing the resolutions for the proclamation of the UN Decade for HRE-Shulamith Koening.

Global Value and Holistic Concept

Human Rights are taken here as a Global Value, applicable and cherished World-wide as a multiple, fundamental base control to the totality of human existence. The attainment of human rights is thus an ideal goal aspiration of pressing urgency, throughout the world. The concept of Human

Rights here is Holistic: composite and all encompassing: it recognises the innate indivisibility, inter-relatedness and interdependence of human life : rights, duties, values, which serve as spring boards for action are fundamentally part of an intrinsic whole.

Representative Centrality

Human Rights Education thus gets a central place: a Representative conscious choice for the achievement of all else that is meaningful to life equity, social justice, human resource development humanitarian law, democracy, peace, rule of law-an enlightened civil global society, ... to replace ignorance, poverty, squalor, disease, violence, discrimination and misery.

Expected Outcomes

In view of the foregoing, the Decade should lead to the realisation of the long-term Vision as a global ideal: An enlightened, enriched, democratically empowered, civil, value based global society. Towards this end, the expected outcomes have in recent years been stated-in various ways, from simple realistic to complicated idealistic terms: such as the introduction of HRE in all educational institutions, formal and non-formal HRE being supported simultaneously by human resource development, poverty alleviation, and empowerment of the workers for sustainable development: emphasis in FIRE and related action on different groups such as children-girl child, women and the tribals across the world. The PDHRE envisions that "all humanity will become human rights literate and participate in the decisions that determine their lives ... We will effect change and celebrate human dignity". WCCI Amritsar Declaration-95, and Palayamkottai pledge-96 promise action and re-new commitment to HR-HRE: also the WCCI World President in 95 asked "Every teacher to become a human rights educator

... so that every learner becomes beneficiary of HRE" . . . and as the moving force of the conference, he emphatically urged each one of us to become a committed champion of HRE.

Expectations

HRE is now being considered a must for every one everywhere with highly 'significant and far-reaching expectations from it:

1. As an agent of change, being an integral part of Education, serve as a catalyst for the attainment of a better world order.
2. As a purveyor of culture: national identities and international solidarity: cultural, religious, social and spiritual heritage of humanity ... living together.
3. As an investment in human resource development: maximise the potential of people in life as a whole.
4. As an instrument of development: overall and sustainable rights, duties, values, social economic, potential, moral, spiritual.

The Right to Life

(Life needs interlinked with Rights, Values and) (Governance Interface of: Life nurturing, protective and threatening factors).

Food: Nourishment, safe drinking water, inadequacy, adulteration, endanger life, cause death.

Health : Hygiene, sanitation, medical care: non-availability, negligence, adulterated and or banned medicines, improper surgery, removal of organs, epidemics threaten life.

Shelter : Place to live, unsafe living on pavements, is

prepared so that the seeds sown grow with the desired fruit. The needed curriculum development exercise must be undertaken as a systematic planned improvement strategy based on accepted foundational principles; and implemented with all the essential inputs.

True Nations have in the Past used the School Systems: To promote a particular ideology and have been successful in their mission, but this was under dictatorial regime with the entire state machinery, including the school, being geared to one over-riding objective, which contributed to the success of the school.

School Level Requisites: It follows then that for achieving the intended purposes of HRE, it should be included as on integral component of the basic core of the entire programme of schooling. The school should practice what it teaches: It must live by HR and Values and demonstrate a culture of HR in its entire functioning. The school HRE endeavour should be reinforced, strengthened by the Home and the community through day-today living, by community agencies and the mass media with proper information, correct representation and appropriate action, setting suitable examples for dealing with concerns and problems related to rights, duties and values.

Higher Levels : During the Decade years and till such time, the school-going generation of today enter college, university, professional institutions.

College/University: As a component of all science, humanities, social sciences and languages, Arts, with a specialisation component for those who may like to take it.

Professional Courses: As a part of the basic-core, compulsory, curriculum integrated with an existing foundational paper or separate units added in all teacher Education and Education-related degree, diplomas, certificate courses.

Professional Courses : As an orientation component in the professional training courses of personnel dealing with human beings, life needs problems, such as, medicine, nursing, architecture, business management, journalism, computer sciences.

(a) Specialised Training Programmes for Services

As an orientation component in National Defence and Police Training Academy Centres.

(b) For Civil Services

As a component of the short-term training, orientation of the new IAS, IPS, IES in time and Central Services enterants. The inclusion of HRE in the curriculum of all educational, professional and training institutions of all kinds at all levels is essential. But by - its very nature curriculum planning and implementation will take some time and more so to show some visible fruit. To complete the inclusion of FIRE as desired will be an achievement in itself. Even so along with it, the need of the hour is for some immediate action with some tangible results in the near future. This means multipronged initiatives through a variety of channels today for a better tomorrow.

Multiple Initiatives

As a strategy of HRE, the urgency and primacy of HRE endeavour, as voiced by all concerned, must be recognised and simultaneous action through parallel, alternative channels attempted for a cumulative effect. School System curriculum planning and implementation: Out of school children and young people in non-formal settings: through programmes specially designed for them ... with more use of the oral, verbal, audio visual. About HR education of parents and community members orientation of all workers in different areas. Non-formal non-conventional methods may be used. Higher Education Professional Courses specialised training for Defence and Civil-Services Senior-junior levels. In service HRE of teachers-related educational workers, school, college, university, levels. HRE orientation of teaching, research and related personnel in professional institutions and specialised training centres for defence and civil services at different levels. Curriculum programme, planning and implementation: In service HRE orientation of practising professionals and those who have already entered the services of different types at both junior and senior levels. Action may be planned and implemented through community agencies, continuing education centres, professional organisations, volunteer groups.

Immediate Prime Goals

UN Decade and Human Rights votaries suggest early action for certain definite purposes, viewed as short-term goals to lead to the realisation of the long-term ideal vision. Here is a statement on some which stand out boldly.

Literacy : Eradication of illiteracy, provision of total literacy not feasible through the school system alone due to limited access: crash programmes, non-formal settings, alternative channels, non-conventional methods.

Information: Widest possible information through educational institutions, alternative channels, all available for techniques.

Awareness : Much emphasised : simultaneously through the educational system, non-formal set ups, community centres and agencies, all available channels, for a, multi media approaches as appropriate.

Knowledge and Understanding **:** Development of common understandings, essentially based on literacy, information and awareness but to be attempted simultaneously as for awareness, people will begin to know and understand, may not be literate in the given sense, but there are non-conventional methods and now the mass media to get messages across.

Empowerment **:** Of weaker sections, field work in progress, credit co-operatives for self-help, different kinds of work opportunities being provided, but new ways and means must be found for the empowerment of the needy in different spheres of life.

Human Development: Full development of human personality based on desirable values, nurtured at home, by the school and the community, facilitated by governing agencies.

Reflection and Action **:** Primarily a function of the major agencies of education training in thought development and the capacity to reflect arid act will be fostered as the UN Decade HRE drive proceeds forward.

Commitment: To rights, duties and values, individual and collective; fostered through the home, the school, the community, the use of all available channels, for a, and techniques, particularly through example and demonstration of committed action.

Solidarity **:** Of people, of peers of families, citizens and communities, of committed leaders to stand together for common human rights, causes on the basis of shared values and help others to do the same ... education system can contribute but essentially it would be of, by and for the people, cultivated as in above particularly by example, demonstrated solidarity of action.

Implementation Enforcement : This is one major factor on which the success of HRE depend : even persons with required qualities may not be able to achieve implementation it has in the hands of others : Enforcement agencies regulate day-to-day life in so many ways. Heightened consciousness without the means of protection and redress may cause unrest, conflict true, committed people prepared to stand together, and make sacrifices may eventually obtain the implementation of right.

Complementary Activities

To strengthen the overall HRE endeavour from different directions with suitable inputs some more supportive activities may be considered.

Establishment of HRE-HR Cells: In educational Institutions Enforcement Agencies to focus attention on HR needs to collect and disseminate information, prepare and distribute materials : collaborate with other agencies: some WCCIAIHRE motivated sponsored ones being established in educational set ups : one police department recently initiated action for an HR Cell.

Celebration of Important Events Days: Involvement of Key Functionaries: Such as the International Human Rights Day and Human Rights activities Birthday jubilees, centenials for their popular appeal, as a rallying point for promotion awareness and solidarity of action: This approach will be quite effective ... with the participation of known HR champions, persons with some kind of star celebrity status and key functionaries dealing with different aspects of HR.

Establish Human Rights Watch : Human Rights Commissions: HRW points, centres should be initiated in addition to HR National and State Commissions, some of which are in the process of being established : these to keep watch on brewing trouble, bring cases to notice of the concerned and raise with the HR Commissions, public authorities, community leaders for the prevention of HR violations and for seeking remedial action.

Thus, as champions of Human Rights and values they build and exercise consensus through networking toward the formulation an implementation of the needed strategy for achieving the goals of the HRE endeavour; and in view of the urgency and primacy of the immediate they act in solidarity to press for even those components of the strategy which are beyond their direct domain but are all the same essential in fulfilling their commitment to Human Rights and Values.

Pragmatic Approach Revisited

The Universal Declaration of Human Rights adopted unanimously by the United Nations on December 10, 1948 was given muscle subsequently in 1976 through the instruments embodied in the covenants on:

(i) Civil and Political Rights, and

(ii) Economic, Social and Cultural Rights.

The fundamental principle of universality in Rights (and Obligations also) rests on the presumption that all peoples are Members of one Human FAMILY "... without distinction of any kind, such as race, colour, sex, language, religion, political or other opinion, national or social origin, property, birth or other status". (Article 2). It is wrong to consider Human Rights as geographically or historically bound say as a Western or American concept imposed on the Asian or other countries. Hence, Rights as well as Obligations must bypass all differences in the human race and justify their universality. The Convention on the Basic Rights of the Child was adopted by the UN in 1989 and sets standards for the protection of children from neglect, abuse and exploitation and emphasises the rights of the child to be assured by the education authorities of a sound education for survival and for socio-cultural development.

The Unesco View

The primary concern in Education is the covenant on socio-cultural rights in an environment wherein civil and political rights are justly evident. The UNESCO spirit is reflected in the recommendation made by UNESCO at a general conference held in Paris in November 1974 while reaffirming the responsibility that education should ensure the promotion of international understanding, co-operation, peace and respect of human rights strongly invites the"... attention of the authorities, departments or bodies responsible for school education, higher education and out-of-school education.. .' for a meaningful course of education in know-how, useful skills, work-attitudes and ethics.

Although half a century has elapsed after the UN unanimously declared and regularly shouted on equality and respect of all human beings on this earth why is the world still in turmoil devaluing the concepts of Human Rights resulting in intra and International conflicts and warfare and human destruction at the expenses of Human Rights and Values and Peace? Why do we see that the more powerful and prosperous nations arid also the big-wigs, the massive political leaders are highly involved in talking 'human rights' yet acting in defiance? The Educators have also to share the blame-why has the UNESCO recommendation made a score of years ago not had an appreciable impact? Why have even the high level practitioners-Academies / Teachers/ Administrators-in education in the general and tertiary systems in schools and universities maintained 'none of my business' attitude leaving the politicians the right to plan and decide and use or misuse education?

To enable us to design a realistic pragmatic approach and a feasible/ possible action process in the SAARC region in particular through Education in its formal and non-formal systems, let us cite some of the main problems that have hampered the growth of human rights in actual practise especially among multi-socio-cultural societies both in the national and global environments. As the causes are numerous and versatile of varied strengths in location and in time in the past, at present and may be in the future, whether in open or hidden conflict, we have briefly listed them arbitrarily under 3 related Heads that are inextricably linked:

(i) *Ps.:* Indisciplined /impolite talk; ignorance of civic consciousness-law abidence/police powers, worker/ trade union unrest, Rivalry by party politics, competition to win only, fragmentation/ separation by majority/ minority ethnic groups, etc. Youth frustration/ unemployment, misuse of political power, bad leadership-national /communal/ Social ... National identity/ patriotic feelings in disuse, Conflicts/Anger mismanaged-destructive tendencies, Violence/ Bureaucrafism/ Commandeering, Clear communication absent, Misunderstanding, mistrust of others, lack of openness in dealings, hasty emotional action . . ., Education too formal not adaptable, creating more separation ...

(ii) *Vs.:* Ignorance of Right and Wrong in situations, Bad examples of Leaders-Politicians, Teachers /

Educator undemocratic Emotional imbalance, lack of mind/character training, Fairplay and acceptance of defeat in dignity not stressed Non-use of Intelligence /patient review/ affective side of education/productive goodwill.

(iii) *Ts.:* One way/sided views, cannot accept losses/defeat, Unaware of appropriate rights and responsibilities, Individuality and competitive spirit spread as opposed to co-operative dealings in diverse situations, Ignorance of how/ when/where to talk/ act respecting rights of others/ can disagree, controlling anger and emotions, Institutional/ classroom education being dogmatic/ one-way information tracks, Multi-cultural problems not reasoned ...

The billion rupee question that affects the Educators is on whether Education as an Instrument/ armament will be able to orientate and lead the young and old and be an asset in Peacemaking and Peace-keeping! Can it assure a job of constructive work in the hour of need as a supplement or if possible as an emerging alternative to the use and/or misuse of militaristic and/or political power? Will the suspicions of the Economists and Budgeteers on accountability in Education in its real timely output as negative, baffle us in finding answers and in convincing the powers that be who allocate the cash and delegate the authority on the question whether Education and functional training can effectively subscribe to national and international reconciliation and the restoration of PEACEFUL living and also the promotion of socio-economic growth?

How will the current constraints to peace amidst the gun-cultures and valueless human behaviour that seem to grow in the multiethnic and other disunited environments orchestrated by political powers/fronts who may be historically/ territorially and socially bound by narrow native beliefs and life styles be reconciled effectively? True Educators have to rethink and accept the responsibility in the name of patriotism and come to the frontline in the parliaments of the people not as mere hangers-on but as Leaders-General; there is a need for a new type of progressive Education system exploiting modern Information technology and appropriately tune the curricula and learning/ teaching process especially to cater to the senior youth in Schools and Universities to suit the needs and times in the classrooms and functionally effective simultaneously at the grassroots by rationalized action in word and more by deed and not begin and end in mere rhetoric and talk-shops.

Initially to find the best answer it is necessary to look at the question in a broader sense. Actually from a less bookish and more a commonsense point of view that affect not only the Learners and Teachers but also the Soldiers and Policemen and Opinion leaders in Parliaments and Subhas who interest closely with the common man. Rather than maintaining a conservative outlook and a status of prestige as a 'not my business' attitude Educators in the formal institutions in School and Universities and in the non-formal education sector in business, economics, legal and other socio-political fields especially those nonaligned to any ideology or 'ism' will have to be motivated through the University/ School (being the, resource centre of planning and may be operations) to win the battle for peace.

Is warfare necessary to make the peace and bring about discipline among human beings as different from enforcing control and training of the four legged creatures? True 'war' is manmade with even educators the scientists/technologists devising the most cruel electronic and nuclear armaments to destroy more of the humans yet in circumstances beyond human control in amicable conflict settlement by cease-fires and peace treaties we may have to accept that war is a necessary evil in some places for sonic of the people for some of the time but not in all places for all the people all the time.

It is possible for Educators to step in and consolidate the peace structures that may have been set up genuinely in a reasonably just atmosphere by the Military and/or Political powers that be and develop a sustainable 'Culture of Peace' by an activity based approach in and out of the classrooms in the formal general and non-formal adult education systems.

Let us look at the question in a still broader sense for Education to be accepted as an effective tool and Educators the best Lieutenants in restoring the Peace that is in pieces. Without getting lost to a battle in words, let us think out the best strategy for the non-fighting actors in the education scenario to give a lead to the young in school, the undergraduates in the universities, the other school leavers and the adults involved in non-formal /temporary training classes to relate to a systematically planned learning programme with a lot of constructive project activities targeted on work interwoven with the concepts of tolerance, understanding, communal integration and tolerance inactive flow in the learning arena; careful planning may be necessary so that the multi-cultural differences can be positively used for a 'one way' system on the attainment of peace and communal harmony in profitable and satisfying ventures so that the multi-sociocultural societies and the majority and minority communities can hope and work out to win together like members of one team in the football field *trying* hard to net the goals through players in the forward, left and right wings and also preventing infiltrations by the opponents of peaceful living from scoring any goals.

One of our chief strategies may be to exploit the sports and aesthetic fields to enable team spirit to flower and also to set the campuses as grounds of peace for trials and practises. It is admitted that although our thoughts are good and VIPs have spoken about them from the highest pedestals in the global and national parliaments, the truth is that in the equation of *'dejure-defacto'* defacto has not been realised.

Thus, there needs to be a strong proposal to accept Education not only as an indispensable socio-economic asset in catering to the Human Capital but also as an effective force for a sustainable Peace, by the cultivation and rapid growth of Values and Behaviour as prescribed in the Universal Conventions of Human Rights and also Obligations of 'man to man'.

4

DEVELOPMENT OF TEACHING OF HUMAN RIGHTS

> "Natural criterion for pedagogy is freedom and only method is experience."
>
> —*Tolstoy*

In fact, teaching plays important role in imparting human rights education in emphatic manner. Here in this chapter we will address the question of development of teaching of human rights education.

Promotion and protection of human rights is a continuing struggle which need to be waged at various fronts. Since human rights are essentially the rights of the people, both as individuals and in groups, there is need for persistence vigilance and living action by the people themselves. Human rights activists, individually or organized in groups (commonly refer to as non-governmental organizations or NGOs), could play and have been playing a significant role in championing the cause of human rights, registering protest against their violations and creating general awareness about the observance of, and respect for human rights. Likewise lawyers, teachers, journalists and professional organizations could contribute their pan.

There are other wide varieties of ways and methods which could be used to seek the objectives. But undoubtedly the most vital contribution that could be made is by having a programme of teaching about human rights at all levels of education. The Universal Declaration of Human Rights (Art. 26.2) gives expression to this proposition when it declares that:

> "Education shall be directed to the full development of the human personality and to the strengthening of respect for human rights and fundamental freedoms. It shall promote understanding, tolerance and friendship among all nations, racial or religious groups..."

The first International Congress on the Teaching of Human Rights (Vienna, 1978) elaborated this point by *inter alia* stating that "human rights education and teaching must aim at fostering the attitudes of tolerance, respect and goodwill towards fellow human being", and that teaching about human rights is a continuing process and should embrace all levels of the educational system from primary school to university level, to professional education as well as out-of-school or university settings. Over the last two decades, programmes for promotion of human rights education have been instituted in almost all countries in Europe, North America, some countries in Latin America and Africa. But precious little has been done in that regard, in Asian countries, including India.

Indeed, in the context of the developing countries, the problem of human rights education has complexities of dimension. In these parts of the world, there are approximately 900 million illiterates; two-third of these are in South-Asian (SAARC) region. India alone has 450 millions of them. In other words, a vast majority of people do not have one of

CONTENTS

and fundamental stages. Elementary Education shall be compulsory.

(2) Technical and professional education shall be made generally available and higher education shall be equally accessible to all on the basis of merit.

(3) Education shall be directed to the full development of the human personality.

(4) Education shall be directed to the strengthening of respect for human rights and fundamental freedoms.

(5) Education shall promote understanding, tolerance and friendship among all nations, racial or religious groups.

(6) Education shall undertake activities for the maintenance of peace.

(7) Parents have a prior right to choose the kind of education that shall be given to their children.

From the above, reference to Article 26, it is clear that all attempts should be made by nations to educate children and youth at various levels and ensure that human rights are understood by the young citizens. Planning of the curriculum, based on objectives and evaluation to test the outcomes, at all levels of education are attempted by institutions of education, under the direction of their respective Governments. Children who go to schools (and are not victims of hindrances preventing them from going to school or continuing their education) and youth, secure education in the formal and the non-formal systems which provide them information found in various disciplines and at best, cognition is developed. Good institutions of education are termed so, because they produce good results and enthusiastic parents willingly part with their funds, to provide education for their wards. Schools which contain renewal inputs are very few and value creation with the objectives of achieving and understanding peace and harmony among people is attempted by them.

Most institutions do not even provide a good system to children, in the absence of which, most children either drop-out of school or come out, with certification, which does not ensure them, any promise for the future. With this background the formal and non-formal education, undertaken by government and aided institutions and voluntary agencies, the need for effective education of Human Rights is advocated.

In the present book we will elucidate the journey of human rights education and training since olden times to the present day when this is needed to make people aware of these. Entire information is furnished in view of recent global trends.

risky temporary dwellings, roofs collapse, walls fall: squalor-pollution, fire ... disease, accidents, death.

Protection : Protection against drinking, smoking and drug addiction: of self peers and others whose actions pollute and harm life. Safeguarding life and dignity: in police stations, prisons, remand home, against torture, harassment, bodily injuries, exploitation. Protection against: terrorist attacks, bomb blasts.

Safety : Safety against crimes in homes, shops, on roads, in trains, streets, buses, leading to loss of life.

Protection of Life : Protection of life against self-destruction, increasing incidence of individuals, students, even family groups . . inability to cope with the demands of life. Poverty alone has in recent years led to a number of suicides of many a person alone, with children or an entire family: poverty alleviation has been stated by UN as a political, economic and moral imperative of the times.

Achieving devised results : Educators are primarily concerned with curriculum and instruction, the educational and training component in schooling. And for HRE, the easiest and most practical way would seem to be included in all educational institutions at different levels across the educational ladder in both formal and non-formal settings. But in order to do so, it is necessary to examine the prevalent situation, determine how it can best be done.

The School Level

It is being argued that school today is overloaded with diverse subjects, the young are not able to cope with the increasing burden of the school bag: as a result the parents and the children suffer stress and strain. Since Independence, a number of new concerns, ideas, areas came up for inclusion in the school curriculum. To mention a few: national values, citizenship education, work experience, skills of learning to learn, life long education, population-family life, environmental education, scientific bent of mind, computer literacy: some of these were added; other incorporated: some grouped for other, somewhat integrated in relevant areas. HR needs a central place in schooling and need to stay there for many more years to come: this entry and exit cannot be of the *ad hoc* kind.

Reinforcement

Traditionally, the home, the school and the church-religious and community setups, have been considered as agents of education. Today the school though a powerful agent, is still only one major force and for FIRE educational objectives to be attained and become operational, the school effort must be reinforced, by all the other forces operating in the environment, particularly, state agencies, community institutions, the home family and the very powerful mass media.

HRE as an Integrated Component, of the Core Curriculum in Schools: Therefore HR must be an important part of the basic core curriculum of a good general education : even so, it must be totally integrated into the entire school program with special emphasis being placed on relevance to day-to-"day living and happenings around with linkages to school-community interaction at local state regional, national, international levels/depending on the age, location, and general knowledge of the learners and access to information of the school. This should constitute a realistic approach, meaningful, responsive and result-oriented.

Systematic Curriculum Development: Implementation towards this goal, the school ground has to be properly the basic right, right to education, which conditions, as it were, all other rights. We very often come across the argument that a majority of the people in Asian countries do not have basic necessities of life, like food, shelter, and clothing; hence, the priority-concern in these countries should be to concentrate on practical efforts for the removed of hunger and other evils of poverty. How human rights teaching', some people ask, was going to help these helpless people? Another point, emphasised is that several countries in Asia, as in other parts of the world, are experiencing turmoil, insurgency, terrorism etc. Therefore, these countries cannot indulge in such theoretical exercise as teaching about human rights.

These arguments may appear plausible to many but a closer look at the realities must lead to a different conclusion. The turmoil and turbulence which some Asian countries are experiencing warrants a compulsory need for human rights education-an education which not only provide understanding of ones own rights (and duties also) and therefore inculcation of self-esteem and recognition of ones own rightful place in society, but also fostering of an attitude of tolerance, goodwill and removal of prejudices towards fellow human beings. It is partly because the educational system did not give attention to the human rights dimension that there is turmoil and turbulance in various countries; of course, there are other variety of factors involved.

Let us look at another aspect of the situation. In most of the Asian countries hierarchical social order unfortunately is still prevalent; while a small percentage of people enjoy privileged positions, comforts and luxuries, majority do not have enough to eat; a comparatively small percentage of students have opportunity to go for higher and professional/ technical education, a vast majority do not. That is why those who are the privileged ones need to be taught human rights to create awareness and recognition of the rights of those who are unfortunate ones and the exploited ones. Let us take the tragedy that was unleashed in Bhopal (India) a decade ago. There were, of course, complexities of factors involved, including negligence on the part of Union Carbide- a transnational corporation. However, it was a grim reminder to us that while the benefits which scientific knowledge and its application through technology have brought to mankind are immense. On the other hand, certain rapid advances in Nuclear Energy, Bio-Chemistry, Biology, and Medicine have posited a threat to human personality and its physical and intellectual integrity and to human environment, it is, therefore, essential that teaching of various disciplines in natural sciences should emphasise that scientific research and its application should be so directed as not to posit a threat it) human dignity and human rights.

Again, day in and day out, we hear about police atrocities, such incidents bring froth a pertinent question. Is'nt it essential that professional training to law enforcement officials should include human rights education? To that extent, should not the administrators, engineers, technocrats, doctors and nurses, acquire, during their training and professional education, the necessary understanding of human rights dimensions involved in the discharge of their duties. This is, of course, not to say that human rights education alone has the answers to all the problems. Nonetheless, if education is to provide the intellectual basis for understanding and resolving important contemporary societal problems, education at all levels will have to deal with teaching about human rights. It is in the context of what is noted above that one can appreciate the significance of the adult education programme. However, education for human rights should logically begin with instructors'/ teachers' training. It is obvious that, however, carefully planned the education programme may be, it will have little impact in the hand necessary information for carrying it out. It is to meet that need that this manual has been designed to provide guidelines for instructors and to help them in choosing ways and means by which human rights issues can be introduced in such programmes.

It should be noted that what is attempted here-does not deal with any established methods of teaching about human rights; indeed, there is no set of scientific methods in this regard. (Perhaps there could be; we do not know yet). It is one field where a teacher's own understanding and initiative regarding how to go about imparting education on human rights would count more than any guidelines. What would make all the difference is the orient at on and understanding of the teacher concerned rather than any specific guidelines for him. For one thing, teaching about human rights does not necessarily mean making students memorize any specific text, say of the Universal Declaration, or any relevant part of a national constitution dealing with human rights. What is essential, is the inculcation of self-esteem as well as an attitude of mind to respect the rights of others, and more importantly, an attitude of tolerance and removal of prejudices. While emphasising the universality of human rights, as spelt out in the Universal Declaration, the International Covenants and other international instrument the programme of teaching needs to be adapted to socio-cultural settings as well as to national and local realities.

It is true that the principles underlying human rights are universal but the approach to real problems, teaching procedures and methods have to remain specific to social conditions in a particular country and a given time. Hence, there can be no such thing as a 'universal' text book on human rights. It is for the teachers in various countries to decide, keeping in view the interest and background of their pupils or students, the methods and contents of human rights teaching. A teacher may take up, as a starting point, some real problems experienced by a community and then draw instances of observance of human rights or their denial; another could begin with inter-community conflicts in a town or the effects of economic recession on a region. This approach in no way limits the possibility of extending the debate to more general questions capable of provoking reflection on tensions which arise when different rights are exercised, for example, application of the right of every individual to education may find itself limited by the prior rights of parents to decide what kind of education to give to their children.

This question is not without important incidental effects, particularly on the rights of females. Indeed, this freedom of choice may operate, even un-be known to parents, to the disadvantage of girls. Certainly, this kind of educational guidance given to girls has structural causes of both cultural and of a social character.

But these causes may also surface in the context of the application of certain rights. As educators, one should know that no good purpose is served by ignoring these tensions. Some may like to initiate the discussion on development of science and technology, how it is bringing the people of the earth to an unprecedented degree of intimacy of contact and interdependence and then introduce the discussion to human rights issues. He may also draw attention to the fact that while much benefits in day-to-day life are obtainable because of development in science and technology, but there are also certain disadvantages accruing therefrom. Moreover, human rights teaching cannot be undertaken in disregard of the fact that some schools arc attended by pupils from well-off backgrounds and others by pupils from under-privileged groups. This is as true for the urban areas as for the rural areas.

Human rights teaching is intended to promote development a process in which the individual is the focus and social justice the goal. Human Rights issues in Asia, as in other parts of the world, are very different from these in industrialized developed society. Here, sheer survival is itself a pressing problem for a majority of the population. For a large number of people, in this part of the world, human rights are related at once to food, shelter, employment and health. What has to be taught and for what purpose, therefore, needs careful analysis in the context of the different socio-political systems. Thus, teachers and adult education organizers have to bear in mind that the best way of making an educational course effective is to ensure that it is rooted in the concrete situations. It should not only refer to principles of human rights but also expose the major factors which impede their realization.

In short, theoretical exposition which is not rooted in concrete social, economic, political and cultural reality can not correspond to the expectations of those who day after day experience injustice and oppression. Indeed, human rights education must also go beyond the portrayal of sufferings. The victims need no teacher to explain what happens when fundamental rights-whether to life, the security and integrity of persons or to minimum economic and social security-are denied. A descriptive emphasis on consequence alone reinforces the state of despair. Rather, the causes of denial or suppression of human rights must be explored with an emphasis on possible remedies.-Further, it is desirable that co-curricular and extra-curricular programmes like the staging of plays, discussions and essay competitions, on themes reflecting human rights problems, should be relied upon as far as practicable.

In addition, human rights education should aim at providing practical experience; as such it is essential that social field-work in neighbouring areas as well as in remote villages should be made a part of adult education programme. A programme for the teaching of human rights, at all levels and in all forms of education, should bear in mind the recommendations made by the International Congress on the Teaching of Human Rights (Vienna, 1978), and the UNESCO International Congress of Human Rights" Teaching, Information, and Documentation, Malta (1987). These principles and considerations that should guide the teaching of human rights include:

(i) Human Rights education and teaching should be based on the principle which underlie the Charter of the United Nations, Universal Declaration of Human Rights, the international covenants on Human Rights and other International Human Rights Instruments, As such, the emphasis should be placed on indivisibility of all human rights— civil and political rights, economic, social, cultural rights, as well as individual and collective rights;

(ii) The concept of human rights should not only be formulated in traditional or classical terms, but should include the historical experience and contribution of all peoples, particularly in relation to major contemporary problems, such as self-determination and elimination of all forms of discrimination and exploitation;

(iii) Human rights education and teaching must aim at:

(a) fostering the attitude of tolerance, respect and solidarity inherent in human rights;

(b) providing knowledge about human rights, in both national and international dimensions, and the Institutions established for their Implementation;

(c) developing the individual awareness of the ways and means by which human rights can be translated into social and political reality at both the national and international levels.

(iv) While education should make the individual aware of his or her own rights, it should, at the same time, instil respect for the rights of others;

(v) Human Right-, education and teaching should stress that a just international economic order is essential to enable all people to enjoy their human rights and to promote and facilitate education on human rights at all levels and in all countries;

(vi) Human rights must be taught at all levels of the educational system, as well as in out-of-school settings, including the family and in continuing education programmes, including literacy and post-literacy programmes.

(vii) In order for the teacher of human rights to be able to carry out his or her task properly, it is particularly important that his or her personal integrity and freedom of expression be guaranteed.

Development of the Teaching of Human Rights

The Commission on Human Rights requested UNESCO "to continue to extend its activities in these fields and, in particular, to encourage teaching and research in human rights in universities and to this end to accelerate the preparation of appropriate material for the teaching of human rights in universities, for the guidance of universities and institutes in which the various legal, scientific, technical and other disciplines are taught".

As regards teaching materials at the university level, a textbook entitled The International Dimensions of Human Rights has been designed in particular for use by law and political science faculties. Steps have been taken for the preparation of a second textbook, on science, technology, and human rights, for use in teaching at university faculties of natural sciences and medicine. In addition, UNESCO has provided financial assistance to institutions in developing countries for the preparation of programmes in the field of international law and human rights. It has also begun the preparation, of a programme designed to intensify teaching and research in international humanitarian law. The Commission on Human Rights took note of the Recommendation Concerning Education for International Understanding, Co-operation and Peace and Education Relating to Human Rights and Fundamental Freedoms which the General Conference of UNESCO had adopted at its eighteenth session. The International Congress on the Teaching of Human Rights, a joint initiative of UNESCO and the Federal Republic of Austria, was held at Vienna from 12 to 16 September

1978. The final document of the Congress comprises two parts and an annex, which contains recommendations and proposals formulated by the Rapporteurs on the basis of proposals by participants and observers. The first part, after referring to the Recommendation concerning Education for International Understanding, Co-operation and Peace and Education Relating to Human Rights and Fundamental Freedoms, enumerates the principles and considerations which should guide the teaching of human rights. The second part suggests

(a) the establishment of a six-year plan for human rights education,

(b) the setting up of a voluntary fund for the development of knowledge of human rights through education and information, and

(c) the making of a preliminary study, with a view to the preparation of a UNESCO convention on human rights teaching and education.

Pursuant to the recommendation adopted at this Congress, a meeting of experts, held at the headquarters of UNESCO, in Paris, from 25 to 28 June 1979, prepared a draft seven-year plan for the development of the teaching of human rights. The draft plan is addressed partly to UNESCO, partly to member States, and partly to non-governmental organizations and specialized institutions. It covers a number of measures relating to the structures, material, curricula and ways and means of human rights teaching. The plan was accepted by the General Conference of UNESCO in resolution 3/03, adopted at its twenty-first session. The activities selected for the development of the teaching of human rights were essentially aimed at broadening or developing, where necessary:

(a) National, regional and international structures for the teaching of human rights, so as to foster the exchange of information in this field;

(b) Teaching materials;

(c) Curricula for both formal and non-formal educational systems;

(d) Teaching methods and the facilities available in this connection.

The programme for human rights teaching includes humanitarian law. In addition, a Voluntary Fund for the development of knowledge of human rights through teaching and information was adopted by the Executive Board at its 108th session. This was designed to provide funds, supplementary to those available under the UNESCO Regular Programme and Budget, for financing the implementation of the Plan for the Development of the Teaching of Human Rights. At its twenty-second session, in 1983, the General Conference of UNESCO adopted resolution 13.5, in which it recognized that UNESCO's Plan for the Development of Human Rights Teaching was one of the organization's major contributions to the promotion of human rights and pointed out that education, teaching and access to education are of particular importance to the promotion of human rights and the rights of peoples.

The Conference invited the Director-General to organize a meeting to examine the Plan and the progress made in implementing it. Pursuant to the resolution, the UNESCO Secretariat undertook a survey of progress by addressing a questionnaire to Member States, international organizations and institutes specialized in human rights research and teaching. To evaluate the state of implementation of the Plan, an Informal Consultation of Experts was organized at UNESCO Headquarters from 9 to 12 July 1985. The view of the experts was that the Plan, originally scheduled for completion in seven years, should be extended and that regional meetings should be organized to assess the progress made.

Encouragement of Human Rights Institutes

In order to encourage the establishment of institutions capable of sustained teaching and research activities relating to human rights, and in order to prepare the establishment of a network of institutions, UNESCO has provided assistance to several international or regional meetings of human rights experts. At the international level, UNESCO has established regular co-operation with the International Institute of Human Rights (Strasbourg).

UNESCO assists in the organization of the annual training sessions of this Institute, and especially in the programme that enables university teachers and professionals to acquire practical knowledge about international protection of human rights. In addition, UNESCO has taken various measures to enable teachers and students to acquire specific knowledge about human rights;

(a) Fellowships have been awarded under the Participation Programme for the initial and advanced training of students;

(b) Each year, at UNESCO headquarters, about fifteen trainees work for a month in the field of human rights. This training enables them to acquire valuable experience, particularly in UNESCO's fields of competence;

(c) A UNESCO Prize for the Teaching of Human Rights was established by decision of the Executive Board at its 104th session. Its purpose is to encourage such teaching and stimulate interest in it. The Prize was awarded for the first time in 1978 and was awarded thereafter in 1979,1981 and 1983.

With regard to the creation of an international clearing house for teaching human rights and for the exchange of information on the curricula and on existing courses and specialized research in the field of human rights, a feasibility study was undertaken by an international non-governmental organization specialized in the field of social science documentation. Another means of international co-operation and exchange of information on human rights teaching is UNESCO's bulletin Teaching of Human Rights which is published with a view to providing liaison between all those involved in teaching and research regarding human rights. UNESCO has published this bulletin since 1980. The topics covered have included: the place of human rights in different cultural and religious traditions; the problems of information in the field of human rights; new issues and concerns in the field of human rights, and new forms of regional co-operation; and reflections on the Universal Declaration of Human Rights which retrace UNESCO's research activities on meaning of human rights.

The most recent issue is a collection of curricula and a compilation of teaching material at all levels of education and on in-and-out of school contexts which will serve as a guidebook for human rights teaching. News from human rights teaching, research and professional associations figures as a regular feature in this bulletin. At the regional level, conferences on the teaching of human rights at university level were organized regularly with a view to encouraging the initiatives taken by national, sub-regional or regional institutes' of human rights: for Asia in 1981 (New Delhi) in co-operation with the Indian National Centre for Human Rights Research and Education, as well as the Human Rights Documentation and Research Centre at Jawaharlal Nehru University; for Latin America in Quito, in 1982 and 1984, in co-operation with the Latin American Association for Human Rights (ALDHU); for Africa in Kinshasa in 1982,1983 and 1985 in co-operation with the *"Centre de recherche interdisciplinaire pour la promotion et protection des droits de I'homme en Afrique centrale"* (CRIDHAC).

Two interregional symposia on human rights were held in Turkey (Istanbul in March 1979 and Ankara in June 1980), in conjunction with the Faculty of Political Science of the University of Ankara. In March 1982, a regional seminar on Human Rights in African Cultural Traditions was organized with the assistance of UNESCO, in co-operation with the Institute of Human Rights and Peace in Dakar, Senegal. In October 1982, UNESCO, under contract to the Association of Young African Lawyers, organized a regional meeting in Lome on human rights within African traditions. At the national level, UNESCO co-operated with professional organizations such as Bar Associations (Paris and Dakar) and research institutes such as the National Institute for Pedagogical Research (Paris), the International Centre of Sociological, Penal and Penitentiary Research Studies (Messina), and the International Institute for Human Rights Studies (Trieste). Several National Commissions were associated with activities to promote the insertion of human rights education in different disciplines and at various levels of education.

Preparation and Dissemination of Teaching Materials

A textbook entitled International Dimensions of Human Rights, intended for the teaching of human rights at the university level, was published in French in 1978 and in Portuguese in 1983. An updated version was published in English in 1982, and in Spanish and Japanese in 1984. The book describes international and regional procedures which existed for the promotion and protection of human rights, and explains how they operated. In addition, UNESCO published a booklet entitled Human Rights: Questions and Answers, elaborated by Leah Levin and illustrated by a famous cartoonist.

The booklet provides answers to a number .of questions about the meaning of the rights proclaimed in the Universal Declaration of Human Rights and about the instruments which exist to guarantee respect for them. The booklet was published in English, French and Spanish. It was issued in

Finnish by the UNESCO Finnish National Commission in 1983, and a German-language version was issued in 1984. Portuguese and Spanish versions are being prepared. With regard to human rights teaching for specific professional groups, a manual for medical students, entitled *Le medecin et les droits de l'homme,* written by Mr. Maurice Torelli, was published with the assistance of UNESCO. A manual of humanitarian law, The International Dimensions of Humanitarian Law, was published in 1986. The anthology of human rights, The Birthright of Man, edited by Jeanne Hersch, which appeared in French in 1968, in English in 1969 and in Spanish in 1973, was out of stock for many years. This publication was re-edited in French in 1984.

Human Rights Training for the Armed Forces

It is essential for the good functioning of the rule of law that the armed forces be bound by the Constitution and other laws of the land, that they answer to the democratic Government and that they are trained in and committed to the principles of human rights and humanitarian law attending their legitimate functions in society. The Centre for Human Rights has carried out a number of training activities for military officers. Certainly, traditional military training has included, in many cases, some attention to the laws of war including the four Geneva Conventions of 12 August 1949. Human rights training per se, however, has been conspicuously absent.

Indeed, not uncommon in some military circles is the notion that human rights training and sensitization are inconsistent with effective military training. Soldiers, for this way of thinking, are warriors, and the waging of war is, by its very nature, contrary to human rights. The Centre's approach to military training takes issue with this notion for two reasons. First, international human rights standards, including but riot always limited to humanitarian law, do apply in situations of armed conflict. Secondly, the duties of modern professional soldiers are not limited to the waging of war. Rather, increasingly, they include civil policing duties, the maintenance of order and public safety under states of emergency, and assignment to international peace-keeping operations. The effective, professional and humane performance of these duties requires a knowledge of and sensitization to human rights standards, as well as the skills to apply them in the daily work of the military.

Human Rights Support to Parliaments

National parliaments have, under the Technical Co-operation Programme, received direct training and other support designed to assist them in carrying out their important human rights functions. This programme component addresses a variety of crucial issues, including information an national human rights legislation, parliamentary human rights committees, ratifications of and accessions to international human rights instruments, and, in general, the role of parliament in promoting and protecting human rights.

Curriculum Development and Education for Human Rights

The Centre for Human Rights is in the process of developing curricula for .education on human rights for the primary secondary and university levels, and for non-formal levels of education. These activities are intended to assist in the building of a human rights culture by encouraging the inclusion of human rights concepts in existing programmes; assisting in the adaptation or modification of curricula where necessary,- and providing instruction and assistance to those persons centrally involved in the human rights education process. There are several means by which these objectives are pursued. The first is teacher training, whereby the Centre offers programmes of training for both primary and secondary school teachers. Courses can also be constructed to accommodate other groups in a position to promote human rights education and sensitize others in this field, such as teacher trainers, directors of schools or teacher-resource centres, and inspectors and teachers within the ministry concerned with curriculum development and education.

Treaty Reporting and International Obligations Training of Government Officials

The Centre for Human Rights regularly organizes training activities to enable government officials to prepare properly reports required under the various international human rights treaties to which their State is a party. In some cases, courses in reporting obligations are offered at the national or regional level. In others, the Centre provides fellowships for government officials to travel to Geneva, where training courses for several countries are held. During these courses, participants are able to take part in workshops with experts from the various treaty-monitoring committees, as well as with relevant staff of the Centre. In some cases, they are given the opportunity to sit as observers during meetings of the treaty bodies themselves. In every case, participants are provided with a copy of the Centre's Manual on Human Rights Reporting.

In accordance with the Centre's standard approach to training, course participants are engaged in practical exercises, which allow them to test the drafting skills imparted during the course. Separate course segments are offered for the International Covenant on Civil and Political Rights, the International Covenant on Economic, Social and Cultural Rights, the Convention on the Rights of the Child; the Convention against Torture and Other Cruel, Inhuman or

Degrading Treatment or Punishment-, the International Convention on the Elimination of All Forms of Racial Discrimination-, the Convention on the Elimination of All Forms of Discrimination against Women; and the International Convention on the Protection of the Rights of All Migrant Workers and Members of Their Families.

Support to NGOs and Civil Society

National and international non-governmental human rights organizations (NGOs) are key actors in the Technical Co-operation Programme. NGOs both assist in the delivery of assistance, and benefit as recipients of it. Thus, in furthering the programme's goal of strengthening civil society, the Centre for Human Rights is increasingly being called upon by Governments and others to provide assistance to national NGOs, in the context of its country activities, by soliciting their input, including them as invites in seminars and training courses, and supporting appropriate projects developed by them.

Information and Documentation Projects

The Technical Co-operation Programme also provides assistance in the form of provision of human rights information and documentation, and the building of capacity to utilize and manage such materials properly. This includes direct provision of documentation, translated where necessary into local languages; training in human rights informatics and assistance in computerization of national and regional human rights offices. Assistance can also be provided to national libraries in acquiring human rights books and documentation, and support can be given for the establishment and functioning of national or regional human rights documentation centres.

Regional Institutions and Activities

The Technical Co-operation Programme also focuses on

the development of human rights infrastructures at the regional level. This is done primarily through the organization of regional workshops and seminars, and through support to regional human rights institutions. The Centre for Human Rights also provides support, through the Voluntary Fund for Technical Co-operation in the Field of Human Rights, for regional human rights institutions involved in educational activities, including direct Support to the African Commission on Human and Peoples' Rights, the Arab Institute of Human Rights.

Peace-keeping and Training of International Civil Servants

The Technical Cooperation Programme has recently expanded its activities, in accordance with the Vienna Declaration and Programme of Action adopted by the World Conference on Human Rights in June 1993, to include human rights support within the United Nations system. In the area of peace-keeping, for example, the programme has already provided various forms of assistance to major United Nations missions in Cambodia, Eritrea, Mozambique, Haiti, South Africa/the countries of the former Yugoslavia, and Angola. Such assistance has included, variously, the provision of human rights information, legislative analysis, training, and advisory services. Efforts are currently under way to conclude a series of agreements with a number of United Nations specialized agencies, the outcome of which is expected to be an increased level of co-operation between the programme and other United Nations organs engaged in human rights-related activities, for example through the provision of human rights training to staff of those agencies.

Under the programme approach of the Centre for Human Rights to the provision of technical assistance, discussed above, the Centre responds to most government requests by conducting a careful assessment of the country's particular human rights assistance needs, Assistance programmes are then designed to address those needs in a comprehensive and coordinated way. Needs-assessment missions conducted by the Centre are typically composed of carefully selected international experts, accompanied by staff of the Technical Cooperation Branch. During such missions, a wide range of parties are consulted in the country, including both governmental and non-governmental organizations and individuals. The Centre also carries out periodic and post-implementation evaluations of country programmes, in order that their effect may be gauged and follow-up plans developed. These activities are seen by the Centre as crucial to ongoing efforts to strengthen and improve the Technical Co-operation Programme.

Human Rights Fellowships

It is pertinent to note that General Assembly resolution 926 (X) of 14 December 1955, which officially established the advisory services programme, made direct provision for human rights fellowships. Under the programme, fellowships are awarded only to candidates nominated by their Governments, and are financed under the regular budget for advisory services. The Secretary-General annually sends out invitations to Member States to submit nominations for fellowships. Governments are reminded that nominees should be directly involved in functions affecting human rights, particularly in the administration of Justice.

The Secretary-General also draws their attention to concerns expressed by the General Assembly, in many of its resolutions, with regard to the rights of women, and encourages the nomination of women candidates, The principle of equitable geographical distribution is taken into account and priority is given to candidates from States which have never benefited from the fellowship programme, or which have not done so in recent years. Participants receive intensive training in a variety of human rights issues. They are encouraged to exchange experience among themselves, and are requested to evaluate the fellowship programme, to present individual oral reports, and to prepare recommendations for their superiors on the basis of information acquired during the programme. Finally, in accordance with the policy and procedure governing the administration of United Nations fellowships, each participant is required to submit a comprehensive final report to the Centre for Human Rights on subjects directly related to their field of activity.

After having a through presentation of development of human right training, now we will focus on human rights education in international perspective in the next chapter.

5

Human Rights Education in International Perspective

> "Natural education, unlike the artificial and formal education of society, enables one to become social, moral and rational while remaining true to one's own nature. If one is educated to be a man, not a priest, a soldier, or an attorney one will be able to do what is needed in any situation."
>
> —*Rousseau*

First it is significant to note that at the national level, the Plan of Action provides for the establishment, on the initiative of Governments or other relevant institutions, of a national committee for human rights education. The Committee should include a broad coalition of governmental and non-governmental actors and should be responsible for developing and implementing a national plan of action for human rights education, with the support of regional and international organizations.

The establishment of a publicly accessible national human rights, resource and training centre for human rights education or the strengthening of existing centres, in support of the work of the national committee, should also be considered a priority issue. In order to support national efforts, in

January 1997 OHCHR convened in Geneva an expert meeting to develop guidelines for national plans of action for human rights education.

The guidelines, which were published in October 1997 and are now being disseminated to all Governments and other interested institutions and organizations, include a set of principles for effective human rights education and a strategy to develop comprehensive (in terms of outreach), effective (in terms of educational strategies) and sustainable (in the long term) national plans of action for human rights education. The Guidelines for National Plans of Action for Human Rights Education are developed in the following sections:

(a) Introduction;

(b) Principles governing a national plan of action for human rights education;

(c) Steps towards a national plan of action for human rights education:

1. Establishing a national committee for human rights education, a coalition of representatives of appropriate governmental agencies, independent human rights national institutions, human rights institute and non-governmental organizations with experience in human rights and human rights education, or with the potential to develop such programmes;
2. Conducting a baseline/needs assessment study on the state of human rights education in the country, including the areas where human rights challenges are greatest, the available level of support and the extent to which the basic elements of a national strategy are already in place;

3. Setting priorities and identifying groups in need of human rights education on the basis of the findings of the baseline study;
4. Developing the national plan including a comprehensive set of objectives, strategies and programmes for human rights education (networking support, institution all organizational support, integration of human rights education into all levels of formal education, education of groups in need, a public awareness campaign, translation/ production/ revision of material, research and evaluation, legislative reform, etc.) and evaluation mechanisms;
5. Implementing the national plan;
6. Reviewing and revising the national plan, ideally involving self-evaluation and independent evaluations, to ensure effective responses to the needs identified by the baseline study.

Currently, comprehensive initiatives within the Decade are being undertaken in various countries. Some examples from various geographical areas follow:

> In the Philippines, a National Plan of Action for human rights education was prepared by the Philippine Commission on Human Rights. The Plan includes clear objectives, target audiences (organized and unorganized elements of society), strategies (trainers' training, organization of networks, integration of human rights in all educational curricula, utilization of village-level officials to reach out at community level, promotional campaigns including artistic and cultural activities, development of monitoring and evaluation systems, etc.) and programmes, including the creation of a

human rights training, documentation and research centre (the Human Rights Academy). In the implementation of the Plan, the Philippine Commission has entered into a number of formal agreements with other national partners for human rights education, to define in detail specific areas of responsibility: these partners include Amnesty International/Philippine Section, the Department of Interior and Local Government, the Liga NG MGA Barangay (an organization of barangay captains or village chiefs), the Department of Justice, the Department of National Defence, the Department of Education, Culture and Sports, and the Commission on Higher Education. This coalition has conducted, since November 1996, consultative workshops to elaborate human rights education plans at the national and regional levels.

In France, a National Committee for Human Rights Education has been established jointly by the National Commission for UNESCO and the National Consultative Commission for Human Rights. It includes representatives from 11 relevant Ministries, namely Justice, Education, Defence, Foreign Affairs, Social Affairs, Interior, Culture, Youth, Humanitarian Action, etc. It is mandated to:

(a) conduct a survey on past/current activities in the area of human rights education;

(b) assess needs;

(c) elaborate a plan of action. Four working groups have been constituted within the Committee to assess the state of human rights education in the following areas: primary and secondary schools; universities and higher education; adult education, including several professional groups (the police, the armed forces, judges, teachers, social workers, etc.); and activities undertaken by NGOs, associations and

> trade unions. Also, a national centre for information on and training in human rights,' publicly accessible and which was provided with a broad range of human rights documentation, was inaugurated in November 1996.

In Uzbekistan, the National Centre for Human Rights has elaborated a national Plan of Action for human rights education and public information. Among the activities included in the Plan are initiatives which address high school and post-high school institutions and the Academy of the Ministry of Interior; seminars for various professional groups, for NGO leaders and on women's rights; translation and publication of UNESCO and OHCHR documents as well as international instruments; and other public information activities, such as the production of brochures, posters, TV shows, etc. This Plan is implemented with the support of the United Nations Development Programme, the Organization for Security and Cooperation in Europe and the Conrad Adenauer Fund.

In Tunisia, a National Commission for human rights education has been established comprising representatives from the Ministries of Education, Higher Education and Scientific Research, Youth and Childhood, Women and the Family, Culture, Information, Health, Justice, Interior and Foreign Affairs, from the Higher Committee for Human Rights and Fundamental Freedom and some non-governmental organizations and associations.

A Human Rights Documentation, Publication, Research and Study Centre has also been established. The National Commission has prepared a report that includes information on all activities implemented throughout Tunisian society for the promotion of human rights.

United Nations activities for the promotion and protection of human rights both as the subject of those rights and as the key actor in their realization.

Accordingly, all partners are called upon to participate in education and public information efforts. For example, by participating in activities of human rights organizations and organizing public events in the community to raise awareness of human rights and of their violations, by making public opinion and institutions aware of the importance of the common framework of the Decade for Human Rights Education and by promoting its goals through the organization of educational programmes.

OHCHR welcomes information on human rights education programmes and materials, and the establishment of a direct dialogue with all interested organizations (providing them, for instance, with specialized human lights publications and documents), in order to expand the network V of the Decade's partners. It is only through joint efforts that United Nations initiatives, to promote human rights will succeed. In this sense, the Decade for Human Rights Education and the commemoration of the 50th Anniversary of the Universal Declaration of Human Rights represent unique opportunities for strengthening the global partnership for human rights.

Education and Other Activities

OHCHR is facilitating, supporting and encouraging commemorative initiatives developed by all partners - Governments, UN Agencies and Programmes, regional organizations, non-governmental organizations, academic institutions and national institutions. Queries raised by those partners are dealt with by the Office on a daily basis. The slogan "All Human Rights for All", and a specific logo, have been developed for all related activities. A special section of the OHCHR website (address: hftp://www.unhchr.ch) has been devoted to the 50th Anniversary of the Universal Declaration: the provision, through this medium, of ideas and information on planned and ongoing commemorative activities throughout the world, is intended to encourage local, national, regional and international initiatives and to facilitate communication and co-operation among all partners. To facilitate information-sharing, OHCHR is also publishing a series of basic information kits entitled 1998 - 50th Anniversary of the Universal Declaration of Human Rights, of which this is the fourth issue. To enhance partnership within the UN system, OHCHR has convened a 50th Anniversary inter-agency task force which has been meeting regularly since late 1997 to discuss individual or joint initiatives in this area. In addition, a specific OHCHR programme for the 50th Anniversary is being implemented, whose major components are:

(a) a human rights education and public information campaign;

(b) support to grass-roots initiatives (ACT project);

(c) commemorative events.

a) Human Rights Education and Public Information Campaign

Since December 1995, OHCHR has been conducting an extensive survey of existing language versions of the Universal Declaration of Human Rights and has encouraged several partners to produce new versions. As at August 1998, the Office had collected more than 215 national and local language versions of the Universal Declaration of Human Rights, as well as some 60 additional versions (in pictorial, audio-visual and other formats). In the context of the commemoration of the 50th Anniversary, the Office is currently making available, as a result of the generous contribution by the Government of San Marino, all the language versions which have been collected; the new OHCHR website page, featuring more than 250 versions, was launched on 10 December 1998.

This project is benefitting from the active involvement of the International Telecommunication Union, the Department of Public Information and its United Nations Information Centres and Services throughout the world, UNDP Offices as well as of several national and local non-governmental organizations which have generously placed their language skills at OHCHR's disposal. In addition, UNESCO and OHCHR have implemented a joint project for the dissemination of the Universal Declaration in schools. Through this project, Ministers of Education have been provided with resource material (including material for producing posters for wide distribution to schools a copy of the poster has been reproduced in A4 format in this information kit) as a means of assisting educational establishments to give human rights education a special focus during 1998. OHCHR is also encouraging Governments to establish and implement national plans of action for human rights education and, in this regard, in collaboration with UNESCO, is disseminating the UN Guidelines for National Plans of Action for Human Rights Education developed to assist Member States in establishing and implementing such plans in a comprehensive (in terms of outreach), effective (in terms of educational strategies) and sustainable (in the long term) manner. In a co-operative effort with human rights education practitioners who were gathered at OHCHR (Geneva) in January 1997, OHCHR compiled the document "More than 50 ideas for commemorating the 50th Anniversary of the Universal Declaration of Human Rights", a list of ideas intended to serve as inspiration for commemorating the anniversary; the document was published in Information Kit 1 on the 50th Anniversary of the UDHR.

The preparation of this fourth issue of the Information Kits, focusing on human rights education, is also to be considered as a means of supporting information on educational activities by all interested partners. Finally, a core kit of OHCHR publications (a selected list is reproduced in this information kit) is being reprinted and disseminated, and new publications are being developed, also in cooperation with the Department of Public Information.

b) Support to Grass-roots Initiatives (ACT Project)

OHCHR has recently launched the pilot phase of the ACT Project (Assisting Communities Together) which is intended to empower organizations and individuals at the local level to undertake activities aimed at strengthening the promotion and protection of human rights in local communities. The ACT Project awards a limited number of small grants (maximum US$2,000 each) to selected applicants. The first phase of the project has been launched in countries which qualify for such assistance in co-operation with the United Nations Development Programme (UNDP). UNDP Resident Representatives, as well as OHCHR field offices, have been provided with ACT Project application material and have been asked to make the applications available as widely as possible. The first round of ACT Project grants was awarded during the last quarter of 1998. Application material and a description of the Project (in English, French and Spanish) can be requested from OHCHR.

c) Commemorative Events

OHCHR has organized, or supported the organization by partners, of many commemorative activities during the meetings of the principal United Nations bodies dealing with human rights. In some cases they have already taken place, while many others are scheduled for the period leading up to 10 December (Commission on Human Rights -March/ April 1998; Sub-Commission on the Prevention of Discrimination and Protection of Minorities, August 1998; and the forthcoming General Assembly).

In the context of the foregoing, OHCHR organized the Forum "Dialogue on Mainstreaming Human Rights in the United Nations", which took place in Geneva on 16 March 1998, following the inaugural meeting of the Commission on Human Rights. The Forum was moderated by the Secretary-General, included the participation of Heads and senior officials of United Nations Agencies and Programmes and focused on the steps which have been taken, and those envisaged, to place human rights on the agenda of the United nations system-wide.

Other past events and activities included round tables and panels, as well as human rights exhibitions and cultural events sponsored by several Member States. The General Assembly held a special plenary meeting on 10 December 1998 to mark the 50th Anniversary: among the various planned events, the Secretary-General awarded the 1998 United Nations Human Rights Prize to individuals or organizations who have made a significant contribution to the promotion and protection of human rights. In addition to the aforementioned events, panels were organized to contribute to the international debate on fundamental human rights issues. Most panels are being hosted by partner agencies, programmes and departments in the United Nations system. Some are also being hosted by Governments, non-governmental organizations or private institutions. The panels are offering an opportunity to outstanding international personalities to engage in a human rights dialogue.

World AIDS Campaign

The theme of the 1997 World AIDS Campaign was "Children Living in a World with AIDS." The focus was on every person under the age of 18 years, in line with the definition of 'child' set out in the United Nations Convention on the Rights of the Child. The guiding principles for the 1997 World AIDS Campaign were in keeping with those set forth in the Convention, and in the 1996-2000 UNAIDS Strategic Plan. For the 1997 World AIDS Campaign, UNAIDS and its co-sponsors produced and disseminated written and visual material and co-ordinated and contributed to activities globally, leading up to World AIDS Day on 1 December. Mention should be made of UNAIDS collaboration with the Fran ois-Xavier Bagnoud Centre for Health and Human Rights /Harvard School of Public Health (a partner organization in the 1997 World AIDS Campaign) which resulted in the development of "Guidelines for Training on Children: HIV/AIDS, Health and Rights".

These Guidelines were prepared for the Regional Conference on AIDS and STDs in Africa. In. 1998, the Campaign is " Force for Change: WORLD AIDS Campaign is with Young People". UNAIDS activities in relation to adolescents will in consequence, continue to be guided by the United Nations Convention tool, the Rights of the Child. Also, in 1998, the theme day of the UN Committee on the Rights of the Child will focus on children, young people and HIV/ ADDS; UNAIDS will provide technical support to the Committee in this regard. Related UNAIDS activities include the preparation and field testing of a model country report under the Convention on the Rights of the Child addressing HIV/ AIDS issues.

Training, Education and Dissemination of Information

Education and dissemination of information through the UNAIDS Best Practices Collection, including information relating to HIV/AIDS and human rights, is a UNAIDS priority, Material is disseminated by the UNAIDS Information Centre at headquarters UNAIDS staff and focal points in the field, co-sponsors and national and regional networks on human rights, ethics and law.

In 1996, UNAIDS published the "UNAIDS Guide to the United Nations Human Rights Machinery" for AIDS service organizations, people Raving with HIV/AIDS and others working in the field of HIV/AIDS and human rights. UNAIDS published a survey of HIV-related human rights activities at country level undertaken by Human Rights Internet, in conjunction with research papers, case studies, background papers and legislative policy-option papers on topics relating to HIV and human rights, ethics and law. The UNAIDS website has a page devoted to human rights, providing information as well as links to relevant material. In 1998, UNAIDS held a training workshop on HIV/AIDS and human rights, ethics and law for legal professionals in Eastern Europe.

Organisation for Security and Co-operation in Europe

The Organization for Security and Co-operation in Europe (OSCE) and its Office for Democratic Institutions and Human Rights (QDIHR) were mandated to participate fully in human rights education by the following OSCE ministerial conference decisions:

At the CSCE Conference on the Human Dimension of the Conference for Security and Co-operation in Europe (CSCE) in Moscow, in October 1991, the participating States:

Affirm(ed) that human rights education is fundamental

and that it is therefore essential that their citizens are educated on human rights and fundamental freedoms;

Recognize(ed) that effective human rights education contributes to combatting intolerance, religious, racial and ethnic prejudice and hatred, including against Roma, xenophobia and anti-Semitism;

Will encourage their competent authorities responsible for education programs to design effective human rights related curricula and, courses for students at all levels, particularly students of law, administration and social sciences as well as those attending military, police and public service schools;

Will encourage organisations and educational establishments to co-operate in drawing up and exchanging human rights programs at the national as well as the international level; (Articles 42.1-42.5);

The Moscow Conference was followed three months later by the decision to develop CSCE institutions and structures. The CSCE Ministers decided, in Prague, to give additional functions to the Office for Free Elections and to call it henceforth the Office for Democratic Institutions and Human Rights. ODIHR was mandated, *inter alia, to:* serve as an institutional framework for sharing and exchanging information on available technical assistance, expertise and national and international programs; to facilitate co-operation in training and education in disciplines relevant to democratic institutions; to work closely with other institutions active in the field of democratic institutions-building and human rights;

The decisions taken at the CSCE Council Meeting in Rome in December 1993, gave the additional concrete task of "disseminating general information on the human dimension and international humanitarian law and requested the ODIHR (to identify and implement co-operation projects with (the recently admitted

> participating States) within the framework of the Program of Co-ordinated support." This programme encourages the participating States "to include representatives of the recently admitted participating States in government-sponsored internship study and training programs,"
>
> Activities organized in this framework include the convening of seminars with all 54 participating States, as well as numerous NGOs and experts, on themes such as: Tolerance; Migrant Workers; the Free Media; Early Warning and Preventive Diplomacy-, Local Democracy; Freedom of Association and NGOs; the Rule of Law and Freedom of Religion. The 1997 seminars were on Election Administration (April) and Women's Participation in the Society. (October). Assessment missions on developing human rights education in the Central Asian Republics, several human rights coursed, and a round table on the mechanisms and institutions for human rights have also been carried out.

As of 1998, ODIHR will only hold one seminar per year. In May 1998, OSCE/ ODIHR, in close co-operation with UNDP, the Council of Europe, the Polish Ombudsman's Office and OHCHR, organized a Human Dimension seminar on the Ombudsman and human rights protection institutions which involved discussion on various issues including the preparation of national human rights education plans.

This was a contribution to the UN Decade for Human Rights Education and two anniversaries: the 50th Anniversary of the Universal Declaration of Human Rights and the 10th Anniversary of the Polish Ombudsman's Office which was the first to be established in Eastern Europe and the CIS. Geographically, ODIHR will focus its future education programme primarily on Central Asia, the Caucasus as well as countries in conflict situations.

The multiphase education programme for Central Asia is carried out with the co-operation of Birmingham University in Britain and the Danish Centre for Human Rights.

Organization of American States (OAS)

The Inter-American Commission on Human Rights has established an Inter-American Programme for a comprehensive approach to Human Rights, emphasizing three areas:

1) dissemination of the Inter-American norms and mechanisms;
2) strengthening national institutions and civil society;
3) education.

The following information regarding the third area - education - is from the Commission's 1997 Annual Report which will be presented to the OAS General Assembly in June 1998.

Education and Training in Human Rights

The objective is to offer courses to the most vulnerable sectors of the population and to create a culture of respect for human rights tolerance and democracy among the population in general. Efforts to meet this mandate include:

a) the Inter-American Institute project for university education in human rights;
b) the Unit for the Promotion of Democracy's programme for education in human rights a programme for the incorporation of human rights in curricula;
c) indigenous peoples and human rights - conducting activities and meetings at national and regional levels in order to train indigenous participants in human rights;

d) migrant populations and those affected by violence - a study of these populations to be undertaken by the Institute;

e) inviting the submission of competitive monographs on the importance , of human rights in the construction of a peaceful and democratic society; and

f) a competition for postgraduate scholarships in human rights.

African Centre for Democracy and Human Rights Studies

The African Centre for Democracy and Human Rights Studies has held numerous conferences, and developed programmes and activities on topics such as: women; management; international human rights procedures as well as education and training. Among the activities of the African Center are: "Civic Education: The African Charter" (Banjul, 6 January 1998); the Working Group on the Additional Protocol to the Rights of Women (Banjul, 26-29 January 1998); a training course in "International Human Rights Protection for Women," (Senegal, 5-9 October 1998); and a course in "International Human Rights Procedures" (Banjul, 25-29 May 1998).

Amnesty International (AI)

In the context of the 50th Anniversary of the Universal Declaration, Amnesty International has taken action to: Invite people worldwide to make a personal pledge to the principles defined in the Universal Declaration of Human Rights-, Work on behalf of human rights defenders who have been targets of human rights abuses due to their efforts to uphold the rights outlined in the Universal Declaration. It is in the context of this effort that AI established Get Up, Sign Up., Under this campaign individuals are asked to sign a text committing them to making a personal effort to uphold the principles of the Universal Declaration. The signatures collected are touring the world in 1998. Members of AI in more than one hundred countries are taking the Get Up, Sign Up! Initiative to their respective countries. Each country is hosting an event in support of the Universal Declaration where signatures for the Get Up, Sign Up campaign will be collected.

For example, AI France has despatched a bus throughout France and Belgium to collect signatures and to provide people with educational material in regard to the Universal Declaration.

Each person who signs onto Get Up, Sign Up! will be given a copy of the Universal Declaration with suggestions as to how they might help human rights defenders. People may also join the Get Up, Sign Up campaign through the AI website.

Arab Institute for Human Rights (AIHR)

The Arab Institute for Human Rights is initiating activities to commemorate the 50th Anniversary of the Universal Declaration. These actions are to be implemented in co-operation with the Arab Lawyers Union, the Arab Organization of Human Rights and other Arab and African national and regional organizations as well as with international bodies. Proposals to Parliaments, Governments and Municipalities:

Parliaments

Creation of parliamentary groups for the promotion and protection of human rights in accordance with the Recommendation of the Inter-parliamentary Council (London, 9 September 1998);

Governments

1. Accession to non-ratified human rights instruments;
2. Creation of national institutions for the promotion and protection of human rights such as Ombudsmen or National Commissions for the promotion and protection of human rights;
3. Creation of national committees for human rights education;
4. Inclusion of human rights in university programmes, particularly in faculties of law;
5. Inclusion of the Universal Declaration of Human Rights in primary and secondary school programmes;
6. Republication and distribution of the Universal Declaration of Human Rights for children (edited by the AIHR);
7. The setting up of human rights libraries in secondary schools and institutions of higher learning;
8. Encouragement for the creation of human rights students' clubs;
9. The release of special stamps dedicated to the Universal Declaration of Human Rights;
10. Media coverage of special programmes and places dedicated to human rights; Municipalities:
11. Inauguration of 10 December 1948 streets in capitals, main cities and towns.

Proposals to Regional Inter-governmental Organizations

The Arab League Education, Culture and Sciences Organisation:

1. To convene an Arab Ministers of Education conference "For the Promotion of a Human Rights Culture".

Initiatives undertaken by the Arab League Education, Culture and Sciences Organization include:

Asian Regional Resource Center for Human Rights Education (ARRC)

1. Training

ARRC will conduct the Training of Trainers (TOT) on a subregional basis and a special Training Course for teachers in Human Rights Education Curriculum Building:

- South Asian TOT for INGO Activists, May 21-25, Kathmandu, Nepal;
- Indo-China Peace Education and Human Rights TOT workshop, September 21-26 Phnom Penh, Cambodia,
- Special regional training on curriculum building: integrating human rights education into formal education, November, Thailand.

2. Publications

- Second publication of New Directory of Human Rights Education in Asia and the Pacific Region, October 1981, - Updated lists of Human Rights Education Material in the Region, December 1998.

3. Campaign in Support of the UN Decade for Human Rights Education -UNDHRE

Regional visual arts competition for children on the CRC: culminating activity in October 1998, Thailand;

First National Consultation of HRE organizations in Cambodia, September 1998;

To co-organize, with Forum-Asia, the National Consultation of Thailand, UNDHRE National Plan of Action, June, 1998.

4. *Documentation Centre*

The ARRC quarterly bulletin entitled "ARRC Post" frequently publishes a special feature on the Human Rights Education initiatives of individuals and organizations advocating Human Rights Education in the region.

5. *Further Initiatives*

- Will continue to collect and disseminate information on HRE material; ARRC homepage in the making',

Promotion of the networking of HIRE experts in the region. Association Latinoamerican Para Los Derechos Humanos (ALDHU)

ALDHU organizes human rights education and training programmes for various target groups in Latin America and the Caribbean, namely—

1. *The Armed Forces, Prison Officials, Security Forces, the Police*

ALDHU is implementing a five-year human rights training programme for the armed forces in Ecuador, Paraguay and Chile; a nine-year training programme for the police in Ecuador and relevant workshops involving police and citizen representatives-, recently, a training programme for prison officials;

2. *Members Of the Legal Profession (Magistrates, Judges, Attorneys, Law Students and Others)*

Training programmes are carried out in Bolivia, Paraguay, Uruguay and Ecuador-, a training programme on the gender dimension for female judges and lawyers in Ecuador and Bolivia and a reform project for criminal law systems have also been developed;

3. Indigenous Communities

ALDHU has developed the "Protection of Amazon" Programme which includes: socio-cultural empowerment, capacity building for bilingual human rights education, development of media and research facilities, organization strengthening, environmental protection and sustainable development research. ALDHU has a page which is released in newspapers in more than 8 countries and on the Internet, and the organization has signed an institutional agreement with the Latin American Press Association; in addition, ALDHU is involved in the implementation of an academic course on Security and Democracy.

Cairoinstitute for Human Rights Studies (CIHRC) Collaboration with UNESCO:

- CIHRS has contributed to the UNESCO preliminary draft of the "Manual for Human Rights Education" and is planning to hold two workshops to evaluate this draft at the request of UNESCO;
- "Human Rights Education and Religious Tolerance": at the invitation of UNESCO, Bahey El-Din Hassan, CIHRS' Director, will give a presentation on this theme on 19 October 1998 within a UNESCO panel on "Human Rights Education' Building a Universal Culture of Human Rights".

Human Rights Training

- CIHRS' second annual Regional Arab Training Course will focus, this year, on "Monitoring the Implementation of Economic and Social Rights". It will be attended by participants from several Arab human rights NGOs;

Carlo Institute for Human Rights Studies

- The 5th annual Summer Educational Course on Human Rights for university students: a two-month course. Human Rights Education Research Projects:
- A research project entitled "Evaluation of al Azhar's (religious education) Curricula from a Human Rights Perspective" has been undertaken. This work commenced in 1996 and is scheduled to be completed by mid 1998;
- CIHRS will issue, this year, a reference text for teachers and school students entitled "The Egyptians' Wisdom," a review of the social and cultural history of Egypt with particular emphasis on the need to nourish the spirit of RELIGIOUS TOLERANCE and acceptance of the other.

Consultation, Dissemination and Promotion

- CIHRS provides consultations on human rights training courses for:
    1. Regional institutions such as the Arab Institute for Human Rights and the Middle East Council of Churches;
    2. Egyptian institutions such as human rights NGOs, churches and development NGOs as well as the Sudanese Human Rights Organization;
- CIHRS offers lectures to churches, developmental and human rights NGOs, where it distributes, free of charge, hundreds of copies of its handbook "An Introduction to Understanding the Human Rights System";
- The Cinema Club for Human Rights offers a monthly

film presentation which is open to the public. Every session usually concludes with a discussion of the film from a human rights perspective-,

- CIHRS continues to publish articles on human rights education in its periodical journal "Rawaq Arabi" and its bulletin "Sawasiah."

Women's Rights Education

- Following the translation into Arabic of the "Manual on Women's Rights" by the Center for Women's Global Leadership, CIHRS will hold two Arab regional workshops to train trainers;
- CIHRS will organize a workshop to review the results and recommendations of its study on human rights education with special emphasis on CEDAW and CRC in Egyptian law schools;
- CIHRS is exploring proposed activities (training research and competitions) for students and teaching staff on CEDAW and CRC

Canadian Human Rights Found (CHRP)

Annual International Human Rights Training Programme (IHRTP): this will take place from June 21 - July 10,1998 at John Abbott College, Ste-Anne de-Bellevue (Qubec);

- Regional Programmes:

Asia - Women Migrant Workers

- a session on training for labour attaches (Manila, Philippines, 28-29 May 1998);
- a workshop by migrant workers' organizations on the International Labour Organization (Manila, Philippines, November 1998):

Central and Eastern Europe - Refugees and Migration

- a workshop on interaction between government structures and NGOs on forced migration issues in Southern Russia (Stavropol, Russia, September 1998);
- a training session for trainers developing human rights education programmes for adults in the non-formal sector (Kyiv, Russia, November 1998);

Africa - Women's Rights

- a week of activities on Women's Rights in Africa, bringing together representatives of Canadian and African women's rights organizations;
- a panel discussion on the implementation of women's rights in Africa prepared and presented by the African organizations taking part in the week of activities;

Programmes by National Institutions

- a regional training, session for official human rights institutions (Tagaytay, Philippines, 8-13 February 1998); a round table discussion involving Canadian governmental and Non-governmental organizations, entitled: "Working with National Human Rights Institutions Overseas: The Role of Canadian Expertise and Resources'.
- a training for trainers session organized jointly with the Indonesian National Commission on Human Rights (Komnas Ham) in order to draft human rights training programmes for the army, the police, religious leaders, educators and NGOs ;

Commission De Derechos Human Nos De Elsalvador (CDHES)

This non-governmental organization is active in three main areas: assistance to victims of torture, legal assistance

-including investigations, on human rights violations - and human rights education in connection with which, in 1992, the organization initiated a programme for human rights promotion, education and training: this has led to the development of a country-wide network of more than 500 human rights trainers. Among the main activities of CDHES for 1998/1999 are:

- the training of trainers;
- promoting special events for the 50th Anniversary (namely, the "Crusade for Human Rights Education" in the squares of the main cities of El Salvador);
- organizing basic human rights courses for community leaders, local authorities, university students and members of gay organizations:
- co-ordinating courses targeted at detainees and prison personnel. Contact:

  Commission de Derechos Humanos de El Salvador (CDHES), Urbanizacion La Esperanza, El Salvador

  Donetsk Human Rights Shools (DHRS)

DHRS is involved in the following activities:

- jointly with the Department of Education of Donetsk Regional State Administration: DHRS is laying the groundwork for a large-scale experiment with respect to civic education in schools and universities;
- the preparation of a series of television programmes on the regional television channel on human rights and civic education-, in addition, DHRS envisages a special programme devoted to the 50th Anniversary of the Universal Declaration of Human Rights on 10th December 1998;
- for September 1998, DHRS is organizing the IV

International Summer School "Education - for Human Rights". DHRS has already received applications for the summer school from potential participants representing 10 CIS and Eastern European countries;

- the convening of a scientific conference devoted to the 50th Anniversary, of the Universal Declaration of Human Rights.

After having a thorough analysis of human rights education in international perspective, now we will turn to the status of HRI in our own country. It is significant to note that India has had a great legacy of hospitality and universal brotherhood. Plenty of such instances are there in our old scriptures. Due to this regard for human values many invaders found safe heaven here and assimilated with Indian culture.

6

Human Rights Education in India

> "The art of education must be significantly raised in all its facets to become a science that is to be built on and proceeds from the deepest knowledge of human nature."
>
> —*Pastalozzi*

It is pertinent to note that Human Rights Education is found to be ingrained in Indian civilisation which adumbrated the concept of *Vasudhaiva Kutumbakam*. The whole world is a family i.e., family is always been a most cherished and abiding institutions in all parts of the world. With the affection and benign guidance of the parents in each family, the young ones are reared and supported during growing up as an ideal human being. Inspite of the onslaught of conflicts both internal and external the family remains a well-knit unit of mankind to ensure and promote happy and harmonious life.

The Constituent Assembly entrusted with the responsibilities of drafting the Constitution of India was engaged in the stupendous task of developing the basic and vital document at a time when the Universal Declaration of Human Rights was adopted by the UN in 1948. The Constituent Assembly took note of the Declaration and incorporated many human rights as Citizens' Fundamental

Rights in the Constitution. Right to Equality before Law (Art. 14), Right to Freedom from discrimination (Art. 15), Right to Freedom of Speech, and Expression (Art. 19), Protection of life and personal liberty (Art. 21) and Prohibition of Employment of Children in Hazardous Occupation (Art. 24) can be mentioned as relevant to the issue.

The Chapter of Fundamental Rights encompasses the entire gamut of civil and political rights including the Right to Judicial Interference. Our Constitution fathers did not stop with the fundamental rights only. The chapter was also included as a Directive Principle of State Policy requiring the state to promote and protest the rights of the most vulnerable sections , of our society. The Directive Principles are meant to give a direction to the policy and actions of the Government so as to progressively realise the objectives of improving the standard of living and quality of life for all its Indian citizens. These chapters taken together substantially contain the essence of human rights and the mode of their realisation as stated in the Declaration of human rights. In a sense, with the Constitutional provisions the centre and state governments have enacted many laws and regulations to preserve and safeguard the basic human rights. For example, Code of Criminal Procedure, Indian Penal Code and the Evidence Act are meant for ensuring human rights of the Indian citizens.

Besides, Government have also setup various national institutes for the promotion and protection of the interest of the most vulnerable sections of the society. These are the National Commission for Scheduled Castes and Scheduled Tribes, National Commission for Women and the Minorities Commission. These Commissions have been reviewing the socio-economic conditions of these groups and related government policies, legislation to ensure that their status in the society can be progressively strengthened through development programmes and by strengthening these national institutes. The National Police Commission and the Law Commission have also made much contributions to the law and order system of the country for protection of the rights and freedom of all citizens.

The Government of India have been continuously reviewing the statutes regarding the rights of the individual. For example, the offences against the members of the Scheduled Castes and Scheduled Tribes, SC and ST (Prevention) of Atrocities Act, 1989 was enacted and therein it is mentioned that if public servants wilfully neglects his duties under the Act, he will be liable for protection and imprisonment. Similarly, provisions have been made under the IPC defining the offence of rape in custody and against the accused. Similarly, Civil Rights Act, 1976, Dowry Prohibition (Amendment) Act, 1986. Probation of Offenders Act and the juvenile justice Act have also been enacted to protect the rights of the most vulnerable sections. Besides, deterrent punishment has been provided for violation of these laws particularly for those who are appointed for protection of such rights.

Our judiciary has the Constitutional mandate to be the custodian of the fundamental rights of the individual and has consistently acted with zeal to protect these rights. Indian judiciary has also evolved a unique legal process known *as "Public Interest Litigation" for initiating* the proceedings for redressal. An individual or group can bring the offence to the attention of the judiciary and High Courts and the Supreme Court of India can take cognizance of such offences and start the judicial process to provide remedial measures. The Parliament and the State legislatures have also been quite vigilant about the violation of human rights. This has helped immensely not only in creating public awareness, but also in ensuring prompt action against those who are guilty of committing such offences.

India also is proud of having an independent and vigilant press which has always acted as a watchdog for the protection of human rights particularly in case of omission and commission of the government functionaries. Discussions on violation of human rights are mainly based on pronouncement of the judiciary and reports in the press. Protection of human rights has also posed a dilemma. On the one hand government have to maintain law and order and on the other to give protection of the life and property to its citizens. But taking action against offenders and culprits very often the allegations are made about the infringement of their rights, particularly J & K, Punjab, Assam and North-East states which are affected with insurgency and such difficulties come to the forefront. Sometimes actions are taken against officers remained in charge of fighting out terrorists on the ground of the excess measures taken by them for maintaining peace and security in this area. Despite all these, the Government is criticised of not being serious about the infringement of human rights.

It is also very difficult to identify the gaps between pronouncement and action, between legislation and its implementation and resolve to act firmly to bridge the gaps. It is also very critical to protect the human rights of the terrorists as citizens of India on the one hand and to take action against them as offenders and culprits on the other. The National Human Rights Commission has been established to deal with the questions of human rights in different parts of the country. Human Rights Commission was meant to cut across various other institutes established under the Constitution and the Law. It would be concerned intimately with the areas of activity which are within the jurisdiction of the State Government.

The former President of India Dr. Shankar Dayal Sharma in a seminar on Human Rights rightly stressed the need for educating the people about the ethics of the country, the universal values and human rights. It was only through such an education that we can create an environment in which human rights violation can be minimised. The former President also emphasised the role of all sections of the society in this task including the government, voluntary organisations; and mass media. Dr. Sharma aptly observed, "We have some miles to go for achieving our objectives of a society in which human rights of every citizen are protected and cherished".

As per the UNO Declaration, December. 10th is being observed as the Human Rights Day in most of the educational institutions for bringing about awareness regarding human rights. On 10th December 1996, the Chairman, National Human Rights Commission, justice Mr. M.N. Venkatachilliah said that *protection from power and protection against power are the basic principles and hallmarks of a civilised society.* He laid stress on Human Rights and the Rule of Law. Commenting on the priorities of the Commission, he observed that children of India should be protected from all kinds of exploitation and be provided with education. Besides, national convention and conferences are held every year to bring about adequate awareness as regards Human Rights. The Associations and Institutions of Human Rights have been active in taking Human Rights Education as one of its important programmes. Dr. Gulab Chaurasia has taken initiative in organising various regional and national conferences in India and abroad. The National Conference on Human Rights and Values held at Mount Abu (Rajasthan) during January 22-25, 1997 is a landmark in this connection and its proceeding has been given separately.

The Universal Declaration of Human Rights calls upon every individual and every institution of society to promote respect for human rights and to strive for their universal and effective recognition. This call was reiterated during the World Conference on Human Rights in 1993 and given an institutional framework with the proclamation of the United Nations Decade for Human Rights Education (1995-2004). During the Decade, Governments, international organizations, national institutions, non-governmental organizations, professional associations, all sectors of civil society and individuals are asked to establish partnerships and to concentrate their efforts on promoting a universal culture of human rights through human rights education, training and public information. The international Plan of Action for the Decade sets out detailed objectives for the international community: the assessment of needs and formulation of effective strategies; the building and strengthening of programmes and capacities for human rights education at the international, regional, national and local levelis-, the co-ordinated development of effective materials; the strengthening of the role and capacity of the mass media; and the global dissemination of the Universal Declaration of Human Rights.

The Decade for Human Rights Education provides us with an important common framework. It focuses on the development and strengthening of comprehensive, effective and sustainable educational programmes at the local, national, regional and international levels, national and local initiatives should be supported and encouraged by the international community. The proclamation of the Decade reaffirms, as already stated in several international human rights instruments/that education in and for human rights is a right in itself, i.e. the right of all to learn about the rights and dignity of all and about means to ensure their respect. This should be our common commitment, since all organizations and individuals have a role to play in the organization of and participation in formal and non-formal human rights education programmes, at all levels of society.

The Universal Declaration of Human Rights and Vienna Declaration and Programme of Action (VDPA) both underline the cardinal importance of human rights education, training and public information - a crucial, enduring, and long-term, contribution to preventing human rights abuses and an investment for achieving a just society The World. Conference on Human Rights reaffirmed in particular that "States are duty-bound to ensure that education is aimed at strengthening the respect of human rights and fundamental freedoms. Education on human rights and the dissemination of proper information, both theoretical and practical, play an important role in the promotion and respect of human rights with regard to all individuals without distinction of any kind such as race, sex, language or religion, and this should be integrated in the education policies at the national as well as international levels.

In response to the appeal by the World Conference, the General Assembly proclaimed the period 1 January 1995 to 31 December 2004 the UN Decade for Human Rights Education. This initiative is aimed at promoting, encouraging and focusing human rights educational activities. A related Plan of Action for the Decade was welcomed by the Assembly, which requested the UN High Commissioner for Human Rights to co-ordinate its implementation. 1998 marks the fourth year of this Decade-, in the year 2000, a mid-term evaluation of progress made towards achieving the Decade's objectives is envisaged. However, some general trends are already evident. While related programmes are being implemented both internationally and nationally, the proclamation of the Decade has not yet been able to mobilize the level of concerted effort called for in the area of human rights education, training and public information - particularly in terms of human and financial resources.

The success of the Decade will require in the coming years a stronger commitment to its objectives on the part of the international community and a strengthening of the partnership between governmental and non-governmental actors. The next issue will focus on human rights defenders. It is fitting that the anniversary year should acquire additional significance as the year in which the final text of the Declaration on Human Rights Defenders was approved by the Commission on Human Rights and submitted to the General Assembly for adoption.

In addition, on 10 December 1998, at the plenary meeting of the General Assembly to commemorate the 50th Anniversary, the Secretary-General will award the United Nations Prize in the Field of Human Rights, in public recognition of the valuable work of human rights defenders and of the international community's gratitude for their commitment to the ongoing work of making all human rights a reality for all people.

1998-Human Rights Year will be marked by the increased and sustained efforts of the international community to:

- Make human rights a reality worldwide
- Prevent human rights violations
- Build a global partnership for human rights
- Make human rights, together with peace, democracy,

and development the.guiding principles of the twenty-first century

Guiding Ideas

1. Respect for the Dignity of All people - The Supreme Goal - all people have the same universal rights, freedom, equality, non-discrimination - the fundamental rights of vulnerable groups: children, minorities, indigenous peoples, refugees, displaced persons, disabled persons and migrant workers.
2. Human Rights - The Common Language of Humanity - building a universal culture of human rights and empowering people - human rights education at all levels and for all people - building a global partnership for human rights - promoting tolerance in the spirit of human rights worldwide.
3. Women Rights - The Responsiblity of all - women's rights are human rights -. combating all forms of violence against women - full participation of women in development - promotion of gender equality - support to NGOs and grass-roots initiatives for the advancement of women's rights.
4. Human Rights, Democracy & Development - Signposts to the Future - right to development - the human person is the central subject of development - elimination of poverty - institutions of democracy and the rule of law - a pluralist society - grass-roots participation.
5. Civil Society - The Driving Force of Human Rights - individual and collective responsibility for human rights - contribution by NGOs in the promotion and protection of all human rights - grass-roots human rights activities - human rights defenders.

people-not merely academics and theoreticians of great renown but also the sensitive, considerate, creative and committed to social justice who will make an earnest endeavour to create something that will endure. Let us give only one example of lack of adequate thought in this regard. One of the worst forms of human rights violations and infringement' of civil liberties is caused by Varnavyavastha (the Varna system)-directly or indirectly. Indeed other widespread abuses like custodial rape, torture, and killing flow from this.

How does one drive home the truth?-the Varna system is fine but untouchability is harmful? Well, even angels should fear to tread on such slippery ground where men like Gandhi and Ambedkar failed. The Constitution of India has prohibited untouchability : 'Untouchability' is abolished and its practice in any form is forbidden (Art. 17 under Fundamental Rights). There is no explanation however about the source of untouchability; and whether or not it is desirable to dismantle it to usher in a society where there will be social justice.

What will be the scenario in a class room where the subject is taught by educators whose concept of social justice in relation to the Varna system is incompatible with what has been stated in the Universal Declaration of Human Rights, or even with the Fundamental Rights and Directive Principles chapters of our Constitution? We saw this during the anti-reservation stir-the English educated middle class and upper middle class intelligentsia in north India [including Marxists, communists and even humanists] had gone berserk over the issue of social justice.

So that the children will be brainwashed by those whose concern for freedom and rights is different from what the Universal Declaration and other covenants have stated. Have we given enough thought to the question that concern for human rights, concern for the individual and his/her freedom is intimately connected with a particular way of life, that is, democratic way of life where the individual is not a mere cog in the wheel but is supreme, or that the dignity of the individual and an authoritarian culture are contradiction in terms; or even that we have inherited a predominantly authoritarian culture on which we have been wanting to graft a democratic system.

We may perhaps recognize the fact that we have not yet prepared the soil-the soil is still not ready to receive the seeds that we want to sow. These are some of the questions which need to be given thought to before we set out to prepare our children to go through a formal course of study on human rights and human dignity.

Instead of having any dialogue with NGOs, the NHRC asked the NCERT to prepare a course of study. The NCERT produced a source book. It contains summaries of relevant portions of our constitution, international covenants, etc. If respect for human rights could be cultivated through these document we would have attained this long ago, for our students have been reading the constitution since the 'fifties! According to the NCERT, "Human Rights Education is not an independent area in the school curriculum but its various aspects and dimensions have been integrated in the curricula of various school subjects and the education materials, particularly text-books based on them." The NCERT has been guided by what has been stated in the National Policy on Education adopted in 1986 (revised in 1992). The NCERT approach should be taken seriously. Instead of introducing a separate subject it might be desirable that school text-books, in all stages, deal with both societal and state violations of human rights.

The NCERT has brought out a large number of text-books on social sciences-civics, history, sociology etc., some of which could be read with profit by human rights educationists and students. But some of the text-books are misleading and the authors tend to indulge in half-truth. Among social reformers apropos of the caste system the authors of the book make reference to Ramanand, Kabir, Shri Chaitanya, Raja Rammohan Roy, Ishwarchandra Vidyasagar, Dayanand Saraswati and Mahatma Gandhi. "Mahatma Gandhi organised movements against caste discrimination". Did all of them fight against the caste system in an organised manner? Definitely, there is a bit of distortion of history here.

Similarily, in another chapter, "Untouchability", the authors write, "As you know, untouchability is a very common term and you also perhaps know what it means". Do girls and boys 12/13 years old know "what it means"? The writers then suddenly introduce the term, "Harijan", but there is no explanation. The writers mention a few names who fought against untouchability, but Dr. Ambedkar's name is not there! (Did anyone fight against untouchability and the caste system more systematically and valiantly than did Dr. Ambedkar? Basically, he was a human rights intellectual-activist).

As suh, merely battling with either human rights violation by the State and to introduce human rights education only in this context, will not do. Nor will it serve any purpose if we confine ourselves to a study of human rights in the legal context only. We have, in our country, highly knowledgeable scholars and academecians who can keep us spellbound for hours by their oratory and erudition-telling us the exact numbers of Covenants, Conventions, Protocols and so on, these are on their finger tips-and how many of them have been signed, how many ratified by different countries. These scholars have given us plenty of reading material on these information related subjects. But do we have material on the ground realities? The fact is that in the context of India the issue of social justice is very important.

To get back to Amartya Sen and the Bharat Ratna, his thesis with regard to basic education has been made to pale into insignificance. Note what Professor Amartya Sen and his co-author Professor Jean Dreze write with regard to the non-implementation of the social welfare programme of basic education (it is their thesis that without universal basic education no development including economic, is possible): "In India, both ancient and modern biases shape our policies reflecting prejudices of class divisions as well as of traditional cultures. The traditionally elitist tendencies of the ruling cultural and religious traditions in India may have added to the political problem. Both Hinduism and Islam have, in different ways, had considerable inclination towards religious elitism, with reliance respectively on Brahmin priests and on powerful Mullahs.

The elitist hold is quite strong in both these religions. This contrasts with the more egalitarian traditions of Buddhism. [There is an obvious reference to the hierarchical caste system], The difficulty in getting even left wing parties interested in combating inequalities in education relates to the general social atmosphere in India including the nature of the leadership of the different parties which take some major disparities as simply given and not particularly worth battling against in view of other-perceived to be more 'pressing—challenges." What are these "pressing challenges"?- We have money for everything, but not for basic education. Professor Sen has a movement, independent of child labour eradication, for implementation of the provision of Article

45 non-implementation of which is a human rights violation. If the point of reference is human rights violation, human rights educationists and violation perpetrated on children by depriving them of their basic right-schooling.

In the context of Article 45 and child labour, there are not many takers for the implementation of Article 45. (Let us not confuse the provisions of Article 45—compulsory basic education to children upto the age of fourteen with literacy, literacy campaign and adult education). Those who maintain that this social welfare programme cannot be implemented for various reasons and yet, at the same time, bring out plans for eradicating child labour, indulge in unalloyed hypocrisy. Child labour is, of course, one of the most atrocious forms of human rights violation. What needs stressing over the years is that deprivation of basic education is also a human rights violation-equally obnoxious and atrocious, if not more.

This second aspect has been almost totally neglected, both by Indian NGOs and those from abroad. They have been concerned, rightly, with child labour; but they have hardly been agitated over non-introduction of universal basic education. Why? This must be investigated by NHRC and others who are engaged in human rights education. They might find that one of the reasons is the middle class mind set which would have taken this violation seriously if the victims belonged to their class-the NGOs too belong to this class; the fact is that the victims, almost all, belong to SC/STs, OBCs, the Muslim minority, and girl children.

The NHRC has recommended implementation of basic education in the context of eradication of child labour, it has taken up the violations of human rights-child labour-seriously and in right earnest. The NHRC should start a movement, independent of child labour eradication, for implementation of the provision of Article 45 non-implementation of which is a human rights violation. If the point of reference is human rights violation, human rights educationists and authorities cannot ignore these aspects. The NHRC recognizes that "it has a special and inescapable responsibility to protect" these "most vulnerable" sections, but does not spell out as to how they propose to go about.

The importance of human rights education is to be recognized in this context. We may take note of what the UN Committee on International Convention on the Elimination of all Forms of Racial Discrimination recommended in 1996 (and India is a signatory): The Committee recommended "a continuing campaign to educate the Indian population on human rights in tune with the Constitution of India and with universal human rights instruments, including the International Convention on the Elimination of All Forms of Racial Discrimination. This should be aimed at eliminating the institutionalized thinking of the high and low caste mentality", We have to V go a little deep-how does one eliminate "institutionalized thinking?" Again, literature produced by NHRC and other educational bodies does not throw much light on this aspect.

Let us be honest with ourselves: we cannot make any headway in transforming society if we do not face these questions boldly. Let us take note of another area. Have we given enough thought to the question that concern for human rights, concern for the individual and his/ her freedom is intimately connected with a particular way of life, that is a democratic way of life where the individual is not a mere cog in the wheel, but is supreme; or that the dignity of the individual and an authoritarian culture are contradiction in terms, or even that we have inherited a predominantly authoritarian culture on which we have been wanting to graft a democratic system? We may perhaps recognize the fact that we have not yet prepared the soil-the soil is still not ready to receive the seeds that the NHRC, the UNESCO, the UGC, the NCERT, have been sowing.

This is what human rights education has to take care of Human rights education must teach us that it is our fundamental right to criticise authority-and in the context of societal violation of human rights, religious scriptures, divinities, avatars, prophets, saints, gurus and of course the holy loafers of our time even though they are patronised by our top ranking politicians. (Criticism does not mean condemnation). The scriptures and the divinities have the divine right to prescribe; but why can't we have the right to at least question them? Not many Hindus would openly question the "absolute truth" reportedly contained in the Vedas, or the Gita, or the great Puranas, or even the Manusmriti. Most Hindus accept Chaitanya and Ramkrishna as avatars; no Muslim can dispute the authority of the Koran or the Prophet; and no Christian will question the authority of the Bible.

Let one refer, as paradigm, to another area involving human rights violation and where tenets of human rights are in contradiction with traditional socio-cultural matrices. Our traditions-Hinduism, Islam, Christianity-see women as inferior to men, often on the authority of divine scriptures and sanctions. According to all socio-cultural traditions women are required to find their fulfillment in motherhood and domesticity. Their duty to render service to the husband, his family, and to his children. In fact some of the scriptures have warned that if women enter public life there will be utter chaos and disaster. We are warned that society will break up if men and women forget the sacredness of marriage. The foundation of society would be shaken, we are warned not only by men but also by highly educated women, if women expressed dissatisfaction at the treatment accorded to them. How does one reconcile all these to the UDHR and our own constitution?

The human rights situation with regard to the woman and the girl child is most depressing. Crimes against them have been on the rise. There has been considerable decline in sex ratio-fewer females than males. Why is it so? This need, research. Why is it that 25% of the girls die before they 'attain the age of 15? If it is malnutrition, then why is it only in the case of the girl child? Why is it, again, that in some parts of the country parents resort to the most inhuman and cruel method to kill girl babies? Not many, not even those women leaders who have been fighting for reservation refer to our religious scriptures that have considerably contributed to gender bias. For example, one scripture sanctions: "Let the bridegroom ask the bride to join him in sacred ritual with the prayer, let our union beget sons only. . .". There was also the tradition of Putreshthi Yagna praying for putra and so on. We do not hear women's organizations demanding the burning of these ugly relics of our past. They are afraid of lie-hunting. Human rights educationists, the NHRC and the National Commission for Women, the Universities, the U.G.C., the NCERT, will have to take up this job of lie hunting which ought to be part of human rights education in India.

They may take note of how a significant section of our opinion makers, both ancient and modern, have contributed towards human rights violations-by rationalising the irrational. They have fabricated many fables about the exalted position of women in our society to convince us and the world portraying them as goddesses. They remain silent on the codes of Manu which have advised men to treat women as their property and slaves; they brush aside the issue by saying that our society is governed not by the codes of Manu but by the Constitution.

Yes, human rights intellectuals and activists do want to revive/create the values of tolerance, non-violence, friendship for all, equality, respect for the human person, human dignity and rights, and freedom-values of which we can be proud. Obviously only that past thereto be revived, and the ugly rest buried, which will help India come into inheritance of the blessings of modern civilization. Which means that human rights educationists must resist the temptation of reviving an imaginary golden age of India's past. To quote Romila Thapar again: "... changes will often involve a basic change of social values. The confrontation can no longer be evaded as it once was by recourse to the theory that our concern has always been only with things spiritual, or by an escape into the past. But the process can be facilitated by an awareness of the past, deriving from a realistic assessment .... It is only the awareness that history is made of an entire people into its total activity, which can bring us nearer to explaining the past in its concrete actuality ".

In the process of reviving our past which can guide us, We should have no hesitation in discarding those aspects which hamper our progress, like, for example, the theory of karma, transmigration of soul, may a, the principle of division of society into castes. This principle took the form which the system of exploitation assumed in the bygone days that was declared to be the creation of God. We must discard that 'spiritualist' culture which seeks to persuade the poor, the depressed, the oppressed, and the exploited to reconcile their lot to suffering, sacrifice, and voluntary poverty-all that signify complete' surrender, and absence of the spirit of revolt. If our human rights educationists cannot take up this aspect we might as well not waste public money. Europe did it by ushering in the movement of Renaissance; we too can if only we shed a bit of our unnecessary arrogance.

"It is an enlightenment that above all the educated middle class need the most if it is to come out of its present state of callous complacency. That this includes middle class students and even children is also granted. It is on the pedagogy needed for this purpose that there are two opposite stand-points, and it is best to be clear about which one is being pursued by those engaged in the, very business of 'human rights education'. One is a pedagogy in which education is considered as an 'extension' activity, trickling down from established institutions of learning and reaching out to the communities, the people and the individual recipient.

The other is a pedagogy that draws upon what is going on among the people-their struggles against hegemony and for due regard and dignity-and to structure the research, the teaching and even the training in the light of such 'education from the bottom up'. It is not until the former pedagogy draws more and more from the knowledge, insights and wisdom of the latter, including some sordid realities learnt from the latter, that genuine enlightenment on human rights and related matters will take place. There, can be no genuine enlightenment (or education) on human rights in the abstract, distilled from 'the ivory towers'. It can only come out of engagement with real life situations; in this case situations of conflict and struggle, of the political process in dealing with them and of the knowledge and understanding that are gained from such engagement."

Professor Sibnarayan Ray's contribution, "Human Rights Education-A Few Reflections" appeared in the October, 1994, issue of *PUCL Bulletin*. Professor Ray raises a number of very

very important questions which must engage the attention of human rights educationists, He writes.

> "Can human rights be learnt and established without confrontation and conflict with vested interests and traditional authorities? In .the past rights have involved major upheavals-social, cultural and politico-economic. Such upheavals are fraught with considerable risks, and often cause much suffering and damage. But can this be altogether avoided? Can piecemeal reform in which common people may take an intelligent and effective part reduce the risk of highly explosive social convulsions? Can such social engineering or experiments in institutional changes be included in a Human Rights Education programme.

All these issues require to be publicly discussed and debated. Not only professional educationists, but social workers, human rights activists and various -other groups and individual's with some awareness of relevant issues and practical experience of working with people would have much to contribute towards evolving an appropriate educational programme. It will be an altogether wrong approach if some central body devises a syllabus and then imposes it on a school system which itself grew up in an authoritarian atmosphere. Human Rights is not an appendage to be added to an already excessively burdensome school curriculum. It may yet revolutionise our tradition-constricted society by first bringing new life into our moribund school system. But is that likely to be allowed or tolerated by the vested interests which are entrenched in the prevailing system? Can Human Rights Education hope to hold on to its objective and succeed without overthrowing the vested interests and radically altering the present system? These are issues which demand open and intelligent public discussion and are not to be settled by any fiat from the centre. What follows is no more than a sketch and broad outlines and a few instances of what have been our heritage, i.e., India's contribution to human rights. Competent researchers can give shape to this sketch.

The first part of the following sketch is a brief summary of a paper, "Human Rights Education India's Heritage" presented at a national workshop. "Human Rights and Societal Changes with reference to SC/STs", jointly organized by DLET and NHRC, 3 and 4 August, 1996, in Chennai. The second part is a brief synopsis of a paper. "Raja Rammohun Roy: The First Human Rights Intellectual-Activist of Modern India", presented at a national seminar on "The Place of Raja Modern India", New Delhi, 10 and 11 February, 1998, organized by Raja Rammohun Roy Library Foundation Silver Jubilee Celebrations. The paper was published in the monthly.

We may start with an account of Buddhism, Jainism, and other scriptures which gave primacy to mail and his welfare and non Sanskritic Hinduism in the medieval period. During the Buddhist period, interest in man, man in his own image and man's affairs on this earth, unlike other worldly interest, became the primary concern of thoughtful men and women. They did not consider this earth as a vale of tears. Buddha rejected the caste system. The basic tenets of Buddhism are non-violence, non-hatred, and friendliness to all. Buddha was a great champion of freedom and tolerance. One of the most significant contributions made by him was the introduction and spread of secular education and education for all.

Bhrigu explains to Bharadvaja: "Brahmins are fair, Kshatriyas are reddish, Vaishas are yellowish, and the Sudras are black". How it is questioned by Bharadvaja is of interest to human rights education: "We all seem to be affected by desire, anger, fear, sorrow, worry, hunger and labour, how do we have caste differences then"?

That in ancient India, the caste system was repudiated is illustrated by a number of characters in the Mahabharata: (1) the marriage of king Yayati, a Kshatriya, and Devayani, a Brahmin; (2) Vidura, one of the wisest men in the Mahabharata and also described as the very incarnation of Dharma, was the soil of a Sudra woman; (3) Vasistha was born of a prostitute; (4) Parashara was born of a Chandala woman. Another questioning from the Bhavishya Purana, "All human beings have the same Father, and children of the same Father cannot have different Castes". The school of philosophy, Lokayata considered physical sense data to be the only source of knowledge. It rejected after-life and reincarnation. We find this rejection in the Ramayana, too.

A Brahmin, Javali advises Rama: "I grieve for those who, abandoning the pleasures of the world, seek to acquire merit for felicity hereafter and sink to an untimely death. I do not grieve for others, men waste food and other precious things by offering them up yearly as sacrifices in honour of their departed ancestors. O Rama, has a dead man ever partaken of food? '. . . O Ramachandra, these scriptural injunctions were laid by learned men, skilled in inducing others to give, and finding other means of obtaining wealth, thus subjugating the simple-minded. Their doctrine is, 'sacrifice, give in charity, consecrate yourselves, undergo austerities and become ascetics, O Rama, be wise, there exists no world but this, that is certain".

According to Prof. Satish Chandra medieval period about non-Vedic sects: "The position of the nath-Panthi siddhas and in Hindu society needs to be understood. Most of them belonged to the low castes, opposed caste-based inequalities, denounced the religion of works favoured by the Brahmins, and did not favour image worship."

The movement, Bhakti has non-aryan roots. According to some scholars it originated in the Dravida country. The works of Alvar saints are important in this regard. Most of these saints came from low castes. At a later stage even high caste people hailed their literature. One Alvar saint, Andal who belonged to a low caste was accepted as a religious leader by the society in general. This movement is characterized by simplicity, directness, preaching and practicing tolerance, love, and friendliness, disregard for caste division, religious rituals and ceremonies. The great scholar Ramanuja, the best known exponent of this movement was influenced and inspired by the works of the Alvars. The interaction of Bhakti and Islam, specially the Sufi ideas, gave rise to a number of progressive movements with the core philosophy of tolerance. In this period, "relations between Islam and the religion,, of South Asia were marked by mutual understanding and tolerance. This spirit was promoted by the rise and spread of Sufi and Bhakti ideas" (Satish Chandra, in Cultural Interaction in South Asia). Namdeva and Tukaram from Maharashtra, the former a tailor, and the latter a peasant madc the Bhakti movement increasingly acceptable to the people: "What can ceremonies do if love awake not in your heart?"

In Bengal the well known Vaishnava poets, Jaidev, Vidvapati, and Chandidas, as also Chaitanya popularised the movement. Ramananda challenged caste divisions, revolted against traditional religious rituals and started preaching in Hindi-Sanskrit was the preserve of the upper castes: "Wherever I go, I see water and stone; but it is You who had filled them all with Your presence. In vain do they seek You in the Vedas" (Granth Saheb). Ravidas, a cobbler and Shaikh Kabira

7

Course Design for Human Rights Education

The Universal Declaration on Human Rights proclaimed and adopted by the United Nations is a historic event that occurred on December 10, 1948. In Teheran, an International Congress on Human Rights was organised in 1968. The UNESCO organised an International Congress in Vienna in 1968 on the teaching of human rights held at Geneva in 1988. At the United Nations World Conference on Human Rights in Vienna in 1993, the drafted declaration ultimately inspired the UN to declares UN Decade For Human Rights Education 1995-2004. Of the 100 clauses in the Programme of Action of Vienna Declaration, four are related to education and training. The World Conference on Human Rights considers human rights education training and public information essential for the promotion and achievement of stable and harmonious relation, understanding, tolerance and peace. States should strive to eradicate illiteracy and should direct education towards the full development of the human personality and to the strengthening of respect for human rights and fundamental freedom.

The World Conference on Human Rights calls on all States and institutions to include human rights, humanitarian law, democracy rule of law as subject in the curricula of all learning institutions in formal and non-formal settings. Human Rights Education should include peace, democracy, development and social justice, as set forth in international and regional human rights instruments in order to achieve common understanding and awareness with a view to strengthening universal commitment to human rights. Taking into account the World Plan of Action on Education for Human Rights and Democracy, adopted in 1993 by the International Congress on Education for Human Rights and Democracy of the UNESCO and other human rights instruments, the World Conference on Human Rights recommends that States develop specific programmes and strategies for ensuring the widest human rights education and dissemination of public information taking particular account of the human rights needs of women.

The Indian Context

The Constituent Assembly entrusted with the responsibility to draft Constitution for independent India was engaged in the stupendous task of constitution making at a time when the Universal Declaration was adopted by the United Nations in 1948. The Constituent Assembly took note of the declaration and incorporated many human rights as citizens' fundamental rights in the Constitution. Right to equality before law (Article 14), right to freedom from discrimination (Article 15), right to freedom of speech and expression (Article 19), Protection of life and personal liberty (Article 21), prohibition of employment of children in hazardous occupations (Article 24) can be mentioned in this regard. The first National Conference on Human Rights was conducted at D.A.V., Public School Faridabad in December 1991. In her message the Executive Director of DHRE, Mr. Shulamith Koenig observed that we are searching to find the ways to exercise the instinctive meaning of human dignity but are not able to close the gap of vision and reality caused by generations of poverty, oppression, illiteracy and deprivation. It is therefore, quite clear that formal and popular education in human rights is a moral imperative and obligation of all teachers.

The Role of WCCI India Chapter

WCCI India Chapter was established in 1987 and has been organising annual conferences at various cities. Gradually the India Chapter Annual Conference has been enlarged to make it a Regional Conference, where all countries in region five participate. WCCI is sponsoring the project on human rights Education which has now become a Regional Project. WCCI Region Five and WCCI-India Chapter have launched an innovative project of sending Goodwill Missions to all countries in Region 5 for promoting WCCI. The Eighth World Conference of education at BBK DAV College for women, Amritsar marks the silver jubilee conference of WCCI held in December 1995 and WCCI Amritsar, Declaration of Human Rights Education was proclaimed.

National Human Rights Commission

The National Human Rights Commission was launched in 1993, and its Chairman Mr. Ranganath Misra said in November, 1994 that the subject of human rights in all its dimensions would find a clear place in the curriculum of some 60 universities from 96. At the primary level about 30 million students would be taught the values of human rights and several steps have been taken in that direction. The Department of Education and National Council of Educational Research and Training were in the process of preparation of drafts.

Efforts of the National Council for Teacher Education

Under the auspices of the National Council for Teacher Education a self-learning module on human rights and national values was released by Justice Ranganath Misra at New Delhi on March 11, 1996. On the same day the first-ever national training programme for key resource persons in human rights got underway About 40 participants from across the country received training. The Asian Institute of Human Rights Education, Bhopal provides work in human rights education.

The Asian Academy of incentives to students and teachers for outstanding Education and Culture is a reputed NGO working since 1979 for the promotion of education, culture, Asian friendship and human rights education in several districts of Madhya Pradesh.

Course Design for Human Rights Education in B.Ed. Programme General Objectives

The teacher trainee:

1. Acquires an awareness of human rights and their significance to every individual.
2. Understands the need to include instruction for human rights and how to impart them in the secondary and higher secondary curriculum.
3. Acquires the ability to organise Co-curricular activities centering round human rights and democratic functioning.
4. Develops active interest in extending guidance for human rights to the community at large.
5. Gets acquainted with the techniques of evaluation to assess the students practice of human rights.

Specific Objectives

1. The teacher trainee traces briefly the events leading to the universal declaration of human rights.

2. Identifies the commonality in human rights and fundamental rights cited in India's Constitution.
3. Explains the need for asserting human rights to members of culturally diverse nations and minority groups within the nations.
4. Lists out points to oppose bonded labour, abuse and exploitation of children, women, tribals and deprived sections of society.
5. Identifies the connection between the concepts of national integration and international understanding.
6. Analyses the circumstances that lead to social unrest, drug addiction, terrorism.
7. Enlists points in support of social responsibility of the government...
8. Takes active part in organising class debates, seminars, discussions on human rights issues.
9. Plans for and participates in role play, dramatisation, composing poetry, songs depicting human rights.
10. Plans for and participates in meetings to observe Human Rights Day, UN Day, International Day of the Disabled, the Aged, Girl-child etc.
11. Collects news items from mass media reporting about violation of human rights and presents them for discussion.
12. Contacts members of the working class, rural people to familiarise them with fundamental rights.
13. Interacts with the peer group, teachers students, neighbours and family members on the rights of the consumer.
14. Identifies situations, ways and means to pass information about human rights to school students.

15. Participates as a member of N.S.S. Community Service in service activities.
16. Gets familiar with the tool and techniques to collect data regarding practice of human rights.
17. Analyses, infers, draws conclusions and reports the observed.
18. Conducts a case study on a chi' labour or a school drop out or female infanticide or unemployed individual.

Teacher educators should always take initiative and make suitable steps to equip both the novices and practitioners of the teaching profession in meeting the challenges of education for a better future. It will be appropriate to recall the preamble of WCCI Constitution which states:

As members of the world community educators have a responsibility to ensure that education contributes to the promotion of equity peace and the universal realisation of human rights. To this end curricular and instructional programmes of all educational enterprises for children, youth or adults should aim to develop in every person self respect, social awareness and-the capacity to participate at all levels of world society from local to global.

Role of Institutions of Higher Education

Human rights are essentially the rights of the people, both as individuals and in groups; persistence vigilance and live actions by the people themselves for protection of human rights are essential. Human rights activists, individually or organized in groups (commonly refer to as NGOs), could play and have been playing a significant role in championing the cause of human rights, registering protest against their violations and creating general awareness about the observance of, and respect for human rights. Likewise, lawyers, teachers, journalists and professional organizations could contribute their part. There are other wide varieties of ways and methods which could be used to seek the objectives. But undoubtedly the most vital contribution that could be made is by having a programme of teaching about human rights at all levels of education. The Universal Declaration of Human Rights (Art. 26.2) gives expression to this proposition when it declares that:

> "Education shall be directed to the full development of the human personality and to the strengthening of respect for human rights and fundamental freedom. It shall promote understanding, tolerance and friendship among all nations, racial or religious groups..."

The first International Congress on the Teaching of Human Rights (Vienna, 1978) elaborated this point by inter alia stating that "human rights education I and teaching must aim at fostering the attitudes of tolerance, respect and goodwill towards fellow human beings", and that teaching about human rights is a continuing process and should embrace all levels of the educational system-from primary school to university level, to professional education as well as out of school or university settings. Indeed, an essential pre-requisite for progressive realization of human rights is popular awareness of and support for universally accepted human rights norms and standards. Teaching of human rights at all levels of education is, of course, essential. However, human rights education in the institutions of higher, learning-universities and institutions providing professional education, has importance of its own.

While teaching at primary and secondary levels or adult literacy or post-adult literacy should not unnecessarily burden the students with specific texts; here the focus should be on inculcating an attitude of self-esteem, respect for ideas and beliefs of other people and plurality of culture and of fostering an attitude of tolerance and removal of prejudices. What is needed at these levels is not so much the question of any specific curriculum-human, rights dimension could be added to the existing curriculum-as of providing orientation programme on human rights for teachers, appropriate school settings and cocurricular activities.

At higher education level we could go further. Here, students have reached, age wise, enough maturity to imbibe the meaning and evolution of the concept of human rights, norms and standards spelled out in various international instruments and also to discuss in depth specific human rights issues in the context of concrete social, economic, political realities with emphasis on struggles, needs and aspirations of the people, Secondly, and more importantly, institutions of higher education produce civil servants, law enforcements officials, lawyers, doctors, scientists, teachers, journalists and so on whose work makes a vital difference in progress of the community, country and society at large.

The underlying assumption, at the level of higher education, is that human rights education would lead to a more enlightened society, and those holding positions or responsibilities would not engage in human rights abuse or to tolerate them on their part in the society/Indeed, those having higher education would be equipped with better capability to resist authority when abused and to promote respect for, and protection of, human rights. Regrettably, while almost all countries of Europe and North America and some in Latin America' have introduced human rights teaching at various levels including higher education, precious little has been done in India. Some abortive attempts have been made here, since 1980s, As a follow-up to the International Congress on Human Rights (Vienna, September 1978) UNESCO addressed communications to governments of various member states requesting that steps be taken, if not already taken, to introduce human rights education at all levels. These educations were passed on the University Grants Commission (UGC), which, in turn, appointed a Commission under the Chairmanship of Justice S.M. Sikri (other members included jurists and senior lawyers) to consider ways and means of promoting human rights teaching in the country at all levels of education. It prepared a blueprint by December 1985 and UGC sent the same to National Council of Educational Research and Training (NCERT), and to various universities; since then the report has been gathering dust.

An attempt to introduce human rights teaching in all Indian universities was also made, in 1985 when a national symposium was convened by Human Rights Centre (HURITER), Jawaharlal Nehru University with the support of National UNESCO Commission and U.G.C.; the then U.G.C. Chairman, Mrs. Madhuri Shah took keen interest and also inaugurated the symposium. Recognising the fact that introduction of new curricula or the revision of the old ones had to be initiated and approved by the academic council and other appropriate bodies of the university concerned, the attempt was to prepare broad guidelines in collaboration with the 'official' representatives of various universities. Subsequently, these representatives could take initiative within the framework of their respective universities, Hence, the Vice-Chancellors were requested to send a senior faculty member, as 'official participant' of the University to the national symposium.

Consequently, senior faculty members representing 29

universities-from Madurai to Warangal to/Delhi and Chandigarh, from Bombay, Pune to Varanasi, to Calcutta and Guwahati, participated in the three-day national symposium. In addition, other participants included eminent human rights activists, educationists, exponents and jurists. Although-the- symposium was supposed to confine its deliberations to human rights education at university (undergraduate) level, but the participants thought it appropriate to cover all levels of education.

Its recommendations covered the entire range of education from primary to V, secondary to higher to university/ professional levels, etc. Subsequently, its recommendations were published' and widely circulated to all universities and educational institutions. Subsequently, it was learnt that participants did attempt to introduce human rights dimension in the curricula of their respective universities. However, there could be no follow-up by the organisers for lack of resources; the UGC did not extend any further support after the retirement of Madhuri Shah, as Chairman, in 1996.

Thus, the initiative, despite wide collaboration obtained, did not move further on the desired course. Of late, there have been much "intellectual" activity— seminars, workshops, studies, reports, etc., as a preliminary, to introduce teaching human rights at various levels of education. Indeed, it is gratifying that there is wider awareness of this need, and that National Human Rights Commission (NHRC) has taken initiative, on priority basis, to promote teaching human rights at various levels. Consequent to its (NHRC) pressure, so it seems, the Ministry and national institutions such as UGC, National Council for Teachers Education (NCTE), have become more active' in 'planning' for teaching human rights. Several universities have introduced courses on "International Human Rights Law". A few universities have also introduced "post-graduate Diploma Course on Human Rights" But the question is: have we made the necessary preparatory work to move ahead on what would be not only long but continuous journey.

While discussing the role of institutions of higher education, it is necessary that we turn to some of the misgivings which are widely prevent including among those who bear the responsibility for conducting higher education-that human rights is *a* Western concept being imposed by the powers-that-be and that, in India, our priorities should be different. This kind of thinking is perhaps partly because Western countries have been increasingly using human rights issue as a political weapon, and also assuming the role of self-appointed guardians of human rights. Thus, partly as a resentment against Western aggressive instance on human rights issues, even highly educated people in India and other non Western countries very often treat human rights issues as one being imposed on them by the West. Another reason seems to be that worldwide movement for human rights is largely controlled by the Western based transnational NGOs. Invariably all of them lay emphasis on civil and political rights, based their reports as if sitting in judgement on the happenings or mishappenings in the non-Western world; economic, social and cultural rights and the factors responsible for their denial and the deeper, structural causes of injustice are ignored.

Further, human rights literature is also dominated by the Western authors who trace the origin of the concept to Greco-Roman period and highlighting, the Western traditions and contributions of Western philosophers. They hardly make even a passing reference to cultures and traditions of other regions. Unfortunately, most of the non-European authors, too, have written their books on material and ideas borrowed from Western authors. This holds true in most of the Indian publications, if not all, on human rights. What is more unfortunate is that one of the premier institutions in India, which prepares textbooks for secondary, higher secondary and senior secondary education has recently brought out a publication, which reproduces text of international legislations, some relevant national legislations and excerpts from the Indian Constitution. It is intended to serve as background informative material for teachers with the purpose of promoting human rights education.

A commendable initiative, indeed. However, the introduction, by a senior faculty member, traces the origin of the concept of human rights beginning the renaissance in Europe and that important landmark in its development are the American Declaration of Independence, the French Declaration and the Bolshevik Revolution in Russia. Indeed, the origin of the concept of human rights could be traced not from any specific period or specific region or culture but from the dawn of civilisation-when human beings first started living in groups.

It should be recalled here that nature has bestowed men with two related characteristics: first, he is an individual, second, he is a social being. No person can be his/ her natural self in solitude; he/she needs fellow human beings around-living in groups or in organised community is natural to him/her. It was but inevitable that at one stage or the other of the evolutionary process, human-persons started living in groups. In all areas and eras, they must have implicitly or explicitly, in legal or social terms, agreed on certain norms of social behaviour, defining the rights and obligations, on the basis particularly nature of socially accepted claims of the individual and restrictions imposed by the need of maintaining social order.

Thus, each civilisation developed its own norms. In India, they found expression in Panchayat system; well defined duties of the ruler and obligations of the ruled. However, here the emphasis was on duties rather than on rights. As Mahatma Gandhi has aptly noted: if everyone performs one's duties, everyone's rights would betaken care of. There is more to the evolutionary process, Human rights basically implies the availability of those conditions which are essential for the development of the innate characteristics which nature has bestowed him/her with as a human being. It also implies basic principle of "live and let live" and respect for other species. Throughout history, India's tradition has been respect for all human beings irrespective of one's religion, race, colour, etc. Vedic philosophy, Buddhism' Christainity Jainism, Islam, Sufism, Sikhism, etc. all lay emphasis on universal brotherhood.

India was perhaps the first country in the world where freedom of religion, freedom of expression accompanied by right to dissent were part of our way of life. In European region, kings fought bloody wars amongst themselves for centuries until freedom of religion and of expression became an accepted norms as late as early 18th century. In brief, the concept of human rights is not the "monopoly" of Western civilisation. Indian traditions and cultures, as of other regions, have made their own contribution to the evolution of the concept. In the evolution of the concept Asian way of life. Its cultures and traditions, especially of China and India had made solid contribution. This aspect is well reflected in the writings of various scholars, both European and non-Europeans.

To cite a ready reference of an article which appeared in SPAN Magazine (New Delhi, September 1995), it carries an article by an eminent American human rights exponent,

Prof. Charles Norchi (Harvard University), who is also Director of one of the oldest human rights NGO based in New York-International League for Human Rights. In that article, the author notes in his concluding observation:

> In the final analysis, human rights is really about human dignity a notion familiar to India's civilisation, centuries before the West was even born.

This is not to say that human rights education should focus on India's contribution alone; this would amount to chauvinism, something which goes against the very concept of human rights, but teachers/students should know that concern for human rights - is not something "foreign" but rooted in India's centuries old history, culture and tradition. Another argument that we come across is that we do not need human rights education. Our priorities, in the present situation should be different; a large segment of the people in India do not have basic necessities of life, like food, shelter, and clothing; hence, the priority-concern should be to concentrate on practical efforts for the removal of hunger, poverty and other social evils. How human rights 'teaching' some people ask, was going to help these helpless people? Another point, emphasised is that India, as several countries in other parts of the world, are experiencing turmoil, insurgency, terrorism, etc.

Therefore, we in India, cannot indulge in such 'theoretical' exercises as teaching about human rights. These arguments may appear plausible to many but a closer look at the realities must lead to a different conclusion. The turmoil and turbulence which these countries are experiencing partly because some aggrieved people feel alienated from society; such a situation warrants a compulsory need for human rights education—an education which not only provides understanding of ones own rights (and duties also) and,

This brings us to the most important pre-requisite: "The teachers, instructors' training and education in human rights education, it is obvious that, however, carefully planned education programme may be, it will have little impact in the hands of the teachers', lacking the necessary motivation, training and informative material for carrying it out. (In teachers' training orientation programme, periodical workshops and seminars on human rights issues could play a purposeful role.) Curricula and the examination system have to constitute the core of human rights teaching, which, of course, remains the exclusive responsibility of the appropriate bodies of higher institutions which should keep in mind that teacher concerned is given wide discretion in picking up specific themes and methods' of teaching, as well as evaluation.

In a general way, some observations are made here. In social sciences and humanities, for instance, introducing a separate compulsory course on human rights should not create much of a problem. Indeed, in some disciplines, such as political science, economics, sociology, law, etc. human rights dimensions could conveniently be added in the existing courses in addition to a separate course. In case of natural science, we know that recent developments in sciences have, of course, brought to mankind immense benefits, but at the same time, this is also true that rapid advances in biochemistry, biology, physics, electronics, medicine and, of course, Nuclear Energy have posed serious threats to human personality and its physical and intellectual integrity As such teaching about human rights in sciences including medical sciences is very much desirable. In the first instance, the role of science needs to be spelled out.

This would involve examples from agriculture, health/ medicine, communications, transport meteorology, etc.

Further, attention to those aspects where the application of science and technology lead to violation of human rights, such as radiation hazards, abuse of drugs, abuse of electronics and computers in violation of the rights of privacy, environmental pollution and ecological imbalance, use of human subjects for experimentation, especially in the fields of medicine and psychology including artificial insemination, manipulation of human embryos, transplantation of organs, pre-natal sex diagnosis, etc.

As regards students of medical sciences, specific attention should be drawn to the "Principles of Medical Ethics" relevant to health personnel, particularly surgeons and physicians as spelled out (on the recommendations of WHO Council for International Organisation of Medical Scientists), by the UN General Assembly Resolution 37/194 (December 1982). As regards training programme of law enforcement officials, besides understanding human rights dimensions of their responsibilities, they should be made aware of Code of Conduct for Law Enforcement officials, Rules Regarding Detention and Treatment of Offenders—Standard Minimum Rules for the Treatment of Prisoners, Standard Minimum Rules for the Administration of Juvenile Justice-adopted by the UN General Assembly, over a period, on the recommendation of various United Nations Congresses on the Prevention of Crime and Treatment of offenders, which meets periodically and in which Indian delegation composed senior law enforcement officials and jurists. Within the limited space it is not possible to go into details.

However, some basic points need to be noted. Firstly, while emphasising the universality of human rights and universal brotherhood, teaching needs to be adopted to socio-cultural settings, as well as to national and local realities. It is true that the principles underlying human rights are universal but teaching would be reduced to theoretical exercise if the approach is not based on real problems; teaching procedures and methods need to be adopted specifically to live problems and to social conditions in a particular country in a given time.

Secondly, there is need for action-oriented research. As we all know, for instance," bonded labour, child tabour have been one of the most perennial evils of our society; the Government has passed a legislation abolishing bonded labour and strict regulations regarding child labour, yet both continue unabated. Then again, bonded labour, is of a different kind; traditional bonded labour in rural areas; then there are bonded labour in urban areas—brick kilns, construction work, glass industries, carpet industries, etc. What is needed is an in-depth research based on fieldwork to bring forth the entire set of problems, both economic and social, which are keeping the continuance of, for instance, bonded labour. What are the socio-economic factors responsible for child labour?

Of late, it is gratifying to note, that various universities have undertaken research work, on human rights problems. At Jawaharlal Nehru University, during the last two decades, more than 20 theses/dissertations on themes relating to human rights have been completed leading to the award of Ph.D./ M.Phil. Degrees. The subject covered range from India and International Covenants on Human Rights, to Child Labour, Rights of the Disabled Persons, Bonded Labour in specific areas and so on. Other universities, such as Delhi University, Bombay University, Guwahati University, Banaras Hindu University, Pune University, Aligarh Muslim University, have encouraged scholars to undertake research work on human rights themes. Research scholars and faculty members have contributed several research articles to various journals and also write-ups on various issues relating to human rights in national and regional newspapers. However, work has progressed in a haphazard manner.

For one thing, a teacher/ supervisor has to keep the interest of students in mind and let him/her to decide about the specific areas of research work. There has been also lack of coordination and exchange of information. As such topics chosen for research projects have been repetitious of the work already done. Thus, several aspects of human rights problems in India, which demand action oriented research, have not been touched upon. It is true that universities should exercise their autonomy but we have to avoid duplication and repetition which sometimes amounts to plagiarism. We have to build-up some research arrangements, as we find in the USA, where all topics, as approved for Ph.D. thesis, submitted should necessarily be accompanied by a 600 words abstract, is also registered with the same Centre. Further, both the list and dissertation abstracts are published periodically. Thus, duplication or repetition of research topics is not permissible. What is important is that micro-filmed text of Ph.D dissertations are conveniently available. Here, in India, perhaps Association of Indian Universities should take initiative in this regard.

Further, for building up a viable and meaningful programme, it is essential that there should be network of documentation/information centres with research facilities at national, regional/state and local levels. Such units/ centres should serve as depository of the texts of international instruments-Declarations, Covenants, adopted by the UN/ UNESCO/ ILO and other international organisations, as also relevant documents and reports prepared by these organisations; such units/centres should collect and disseminate information on national and international human rights legislations, as well as information relating to syllabic materials and instructional guides for all levels of education and availability of material towards setting of priorities for effective human right research. It is also necessary that these units/ centres should function as an autonomous unit/ centre and not as part of the general library. Documentation system and cataloguing of human rights material is very different from that of a library.

Documentation Centre in-charge should be one who has excellent knowledge of human rights material, including the material published by UNESCO and the United Nations. What is more important is that he should be familiar with human rights information and documentation system as spelled out by HURIDOCS International. Needless to say, we have yet to make a beginning in the desired direction. Curricula in various disciplines have to be restructured, reading material has to be prepared, programmes for cocurricular, extracurricular activities for promotion of human rights education have to be introduced. What is perhaps most important is orientation and training programme of teachers-motivated and dedicated to the promotion of respect for and awareness of human rights and also well equipped with necessary informative material.

8

Human Rights Education in Teachers Training Programme

As is obvious from the analysis of human rights education in preceding chapters, this has become an integral part of education from primary level to the higher education.

Now in the curricular of various teachers training programmes—be they degree or diploma—human rights education is being included as a paper. Here in this chapter we shall discuss the utility and relevance of the same.

The inherent insecurity and a sense of self-gratification has urged men to dominate and subjugate the meeker human beings which inevitably led to conflicts, struggles, strife and wars among tribes, ethnic groups, races and nations since time immemorial. Wherever one goes in the world, it doesn't matter where, one finds that society is in a perpetual state of conflict. There are always the powerful, the rich on one hand and the poor on the other and each one is enviously competing for a higher position, more power and greater prestige. That is the state of the world and so there is always war going on both within and without.

Now if you and I want to bring about a complete revolution in the social order, the first thing we have to understand is the instinct for the acquisition of power. Most of us want power in one form or another. We think we shall achieve that which is good through power, but the very pursuit of power-power for ourselves, power for ones own country, power of an ideology-is evil, destructive, because it inevitably creates opposing powers, and so there is always conflict. Is it not right then, that education should help us, as we grow up, to perceive the importance of bringing about a world in which there is no conflict. A world in which you are not in conflict with your neighbour or with any group of people, because the drive and ambition which is the desire for position and power, has utterly ceased. The growing realization to put a check on all kinds of exploitations and assaults on human dignity focuses on the ensuring of Human Rights to all.

The human rights consciousness, that the Magna Carta imparted in 1215 AD, provoked the human conscience else where. Provocative social elements in the West awakened the masses to rise to the occasion of American, French and Russian revolutions, which in the aftermath, had laid down the fundamental human rights in a firm canvas. The doctrines of liberty equality, justice and exploitation free society became the bedrock of modem world view. The twentieth century also saw the two most devastating wars in human history The holocaust of World War II had further taught mankind the dire consequences the world had faced by transgression of established norms of human rights.

Hence the United Nations firm commitment towards protection of human rights and maintenance of peace and security in the world as expressed in the Charter of United Nations. It is from the UN-Human Rights relationship that the Human Rights jurisprudence has been gradually restructured and evolved. On the 10th of December 1948 the

Universal Declaration of Human Rights which was proclaimed in a little over three years after the UN Charter is an elaborate list of human rights intended as a common standard of achievement for all peoples and all nations. Hence it influenced the constitutions and legal systems of many countries. The Universal Declaration was followed by many other declarations subsequently like an International Congress on Human Rights in Teheran in 1968, International Congress in Vienna organised by UNESCO in 1978, seminar on the teachings of Human Rights at Geneva in 1988 and United Nations World Conference on Human Rights in Vienna in 1993 which inspired the UN to declare UN Decade for Human Rights Education from 1995 to 2004. Out of the 100 clauses in the Programme of Action of Vienna Declaration, four are related to Education and Training.

When our Constitution was being drafted the Universal Declaration of Human Rights (1948) was proclaimed and the Constituent Assembly incorporated many Human Rights in the form of fundamental rights of the citizens in our Constitution like the right to equality before law, freedom from discrimination, freedom of speech and expression and prohibition of employment of children in hazardous occupation etc.

World Council for Curriculum and Instruction

Many NGOs also took up this cause like WCCI under the able leadership of Dr. Gulab Chaurasia who organised many National and International Conferences on Human Rights Education and published Handbooks, Guidelines, newsletters for the guidance of all workers and Resource persons in Human Rights Education. National Human Rights Commission and States V Human Rights Commissions: "The National Human Rights Commission was constituted in October 1993 under the Human Rights Ordinance on 28

September 1993 which was soon after ended as the "Protection of Human Rights Act, 1993". It is a fully autonomous body.

All Human Rights documents give a prominent place to Rights to Education. They also stress the importance of education in promoting human rights. UNESCO has played a leading role in promoting education in human rights and issued comprehensive recommendations dealing with various aspects of education in human rights in Nov. 1974. A world plan of Action on Education for Human Rights and Democracy was adopted in March 1993 by the International Congress on Education for Human Rights and Democracy in Montreal (Canada). It emphasized that human rights education must be viewed as an exercise in democracy and teaching of Human Rights and Democracy should be included in the curricula at all levels of the school system.

National Policy on Education and Human Rights

The reports of various Education Commissions and statements of educational policy in India have articulated the importance of the Rights to Education and Education in Human Rights as a part of the effort for the reform and development of education in India, Some paras of the National Policy on Education which was adopted by India's Parliament in 1986 emphasize on certain aspects of the content and process that have a bearing on education in Human Rights, It has laid special stress on National System of Education, for equality with special reference to women, scheduled castes, scheduled tribes, minorities, handicapped and value education.

Under the initiative of the National Council of Teacher Education, a self-learning module on Human Rights and National values was released by Justice Ranganath Mishra at New Delhi on March 11,1996. On this very day the first ever National Training Programme for key resource persons in human rights got underway About 40 persons received training from across the country In this National Seminar held at NCTE-New Delhi, Dr. Gulab Chaurasia in his paper stressed the need to develop curriculum for all stages of education to incorporate Human Rights, Humanitarian Law, Democracy, Peace and Social justice. He reiterated that in order to accomplish this tremendous task we have to look into the preparation of instructional material, teaching aids and teaching guides, etc. The University of Bombay has decided to introduce a one year post-graduate course in Human Rights.

The Need of Including Human Rights Education in B.Ed. Course

In order to introduce Human Rights Education in the curricula at all levels of the school we will first of all have to educate our B.Ed students so that they can efficiently educate their students later on. Some States in India have already included Human Rights Education in their B.Ed course but NCTE should ensure that it is a part of the curriculum of B.Ed, all over they country. For this some seminars of Teacher Educators should be organised by NCTE in order to train them first as resource persons. In order to make the teacher trainees aware of human rights and their significance in life they should be imparted education not only theoretically but also by organizing curricular activities. Besides giving the theoretical knowledge of the various declarations the students can be taken to places where human rights are abused like Bonded labour, child labour, tribal and deprived sections of society and allow them to communicate with them on their own level.

Activities of N.S.S., girl guiding should allow the students to analyse the circumstances that lead to social unrest, drug-addiction and terrorism, etc. and then enlist the points of social responsibilities of the Government. They can organise and participate in street plays, debates, seminars, discussions and composing poems on the issues of human rights. Active participation and celebration of important days like: UN day, Human Rights Day, International days of the disabled, the aged and girl child, etc. Collect news items from mass media about violation of human rights and voice against it in public. Interact with labour class, with rural people, backward people and familiarize them with the fundamental rights of the citizens of India. Identify the connection between the concepts of national integration and international understanding. They can conduct case studies on child labour or school dropout or a case of female infanticide and analyse, infer and draw conclusions from it. For this they will also need to get familiar with the tools and techniques of collecting data and knowledge of research methodology etc. In morning assembly sessions brief presentations can be made by members of human rights education clubs in the college campus. Social service club can also hold exhibitions and education projects to improve the lot of the less fortunate. Workshops should be organised to study the already existing course of human rights education for B.Ed, students and suggestions should by welcomed by experts and in the end a report should be prepared and submitted suggesting the content and methodology of human rights education for B.Ed, students.

Teaching at all Levels Professional Education

The teaching of human rights as a topic has been permanently present in several teachers' seminars and other conferences for educators sponsored by national and international organizations since 1948. At the "International Seminar on the Teaching of Human Rights" in Geneva,

1988, Mr. Vasak outlined in his paper the historic development of the teaching of human rights. Milestones in this history were the adoption of the Universal Declaration of Human Rights in 1948, the International Year of Human Rights in 1968 with the Teheran Conference and the international community's acknowledge of the efforts being made for the development of the understanding of human rights through teaching; then in 1969, the foundation of the International Institute for Human Rights in Strasburg, which established training and teaching as means of promoting human rights and, in 1978, an International Congress organized by UNESCO on the teaching of human rights".

Education is part of the triangular relationship that Mr. Jan Martenson has pointed out as existing between legislation, implementation, and information/ education. He stresses the need for everyone, everywhere, to know about his or her own rights as an essential element towards the universal implementation of human rights norms, and has also referred to the possibility that the international community might soon launch a world public information campaign-for human rights, engaging the complementary activities of the United Nations system, governments, and non-governmental organizations. It could be argued that much has been said, commented, discussed and proposed in relation to human rights. However, there is an aspect which has not received enough attention, namely, the curriculum of human rights as a subject. Indeed, we have not delved deeply into the curriculum contents of human rights.

We have not given satisfactory answers in relation to the criteria to be handled in the selection and organization of such contents, Moreover, we have plenty of questions related to the process of transference or "teaching" of these contents, and above all, about the variety of meanings that students may give to such knowledge and the different ways the intake process may have. In previous works' some reflections have already been put forward in this direction. In this paper, we shall attempt to analyse the most relevant and controversial aspects of the human rights curriculum. Such analysis can certainly not be exhausted in one paper, but it is essential if we are to make suggestions towards a methodology in the teaching of human rights. In other words, we argue that there is a dependent relationship between the content of human rights and the different ways and methodologies used in their teaching. The very nature of the human rights contents leads us to selection of teaching methods which agree with the meanings such contents are associated with.

When thinking about the curriculum, the first question that comes to our mind is in what way be the knowledge of human rights can be structured and elaborated at school level. As any other knowledge, that of human rights is a, social and historic product. Therefore, inspite of the universal character human rights have, they adopt different meanings and connotations in different societies., cultures and peoples. At school, too, this knowledge becomes truly meaningful only in the teachers' and students' minds. There, it transforms itself and becomes objective.

The concept of human rights will have a different meaning, in, say, a shanty town school-where violations are part of everyday life-from that given in a middle class school. Likewise, the connotation will be different in today's Chile, emerging to democracy after a bloody dictatorship where human rights were systematically and officially infringed upon, from those countries where human rights are part of every citizen's culture. We concepulize the content of human rights as a kind of knowledge which is not necessarily classified, structured or codified by someone else's understanding or in someone else's actions regardless of the values these codes and structures may have. On the contrary, we understand that such content arises rationally from the person and collective experience of the learner and in his or her everyday life and environment.

Hence, we are more interested in the actual process of production and construction of the human rights contents and knowledge than we are in its reproduction. The meanings given by the students themselves arising from their own codes matter more than imposed, external symbolism. The latter does not mean that the accumulated and systematic knowledge of the topic should be left out of the curriculum, but, this knowledge is reshaped in the meaning students give to their own experience and the way they systematize it. It should also he mentioned that the human rights contents are not to be found in the syllabus, study programmes and school texts alone. They also reveal themselves in the way these contents are conveyed, in the emotional atmosphere of the school, and in the variety of communicative exchanges. In other words, the human right's meanings are not fully exhausted in the open curriculum of the School.

On the contrary, they acquire due relevance in the hidden curriculum. The hidden curriculum is revealed in the creation of a "school atmosphere" which truly reflects the respect for and the promotion of human rights in the School's everyday activities. It is, thus, associated with school culture where human rights are deeply rooted in the school's everyday life. The need arises to integrate values, attitudes, knowledge, and patterns of behaviour into the student's personal experience, that is to say, to understand reality with a critical view, and to develop a set of behaviours which should lead towards conscious action. In that respect,

assumes the contradictions implied in the political and social contexts in relation to the acceptance and full realization of human rights. The teaching methodologies in the attitude-value area find their source in those fields related to personal growth, humanist education, student-centered non-directive systems, self-management methodologies, techniques for the development of consciousness etc. Because of the critical component and the need to elaborate transforming postulates of society where thought and action are dialectally interrelated, it is of the utmost importance in the formation or attitudes and the, internationalization of values for human rights, to propose methodologies which integrate both the cognitive and affective elements on the one hand, and personal and social aspects on the other. In this sense, our proposal is close to the "confluential methodologies" and the "Freire's methodologies".

c) ***Finally,*** the learning area of behaviour and action which is, needless to say, the one where conceptual language and acquired attitudes and values become active. The first two kinds of learning would be meaningless if they did not show up in a consistent behaviour. However, it is important to point out that action is a kind of learning with its own identity, Therefore, it does not follow that once a proper conceptual language and the relevant values and attitudes have been learned, *the* learning for action in human rights will be automatically achieved. It is necessary to direct the learning for action through the creation of adequate conditions for the student to exercise human rights.

The various kinds of behaviour related to human rights that students can practise in schools exceed the possibilities of any curriculum; therefore, the practice should be closely tied to the student's everyday life, his or her daily needs and the needs of his or her family

> find social environment, these are fundamental resorts to learn and practise action behaviour in human rights. The field work methodologies in which students are actively and critically exposed to the serious problems human rights face both inside and outside school are considered relevant and adequate. Through these methodologies, students learn how to act in order to encourage respect for and practice of human rights in their school and communities.

A classical question about curriculum deals with the criteria handled to include certain cultural areas in the curriculum while excluding others. Referred to human rights, this question is very difficult. The main difficulty lies on the fact that "all fundamental rights and liberties are indivisible and interdependent". Thus, equal and urgent attention should be paid to their recognition, introduction, promotion, and protection".

Moreover, it is held that "all human rights have, for ontological and material reasons, the same nature, although they might have a different character and different protection systems. No hierarchy among them is acceptable; nor can be accepted as licit the violation or ignorance of one category of rights under the excuse that another claims priority". This wide, interdependent, indivisible character of human rights is, undoubtedly, a problem for the curriculum. Nevertheless, this very character can be helpful for the use of integrating methodologies which, making use of dialectical approaches, relate different concepts involved in human rights. The dialectical aspect has been understood as the process by means of which contradictions are solved through their integration in more comprehensive systems which represent a "higher level of truth".

That is how for instance, the dialectic between peace,

Human Rights and Development means that the proposition which states that one of these three concepts have priority above the other two is to be replaced by three reciprocally compatible propositions in which each of the members of this triad (Peace.. Human Rights and Development) can be achieved only if the other two are also achieved. In this way, none of these concepts can be considered in isolation. With regard to the organization of contents, the debate has preferably tackled the problem of the place and amount of time devoted for human rights in the curriculum. Some favour the position that Human Rights should be a study subject the same as Mathematics, Science or History. They argue that this is the only possible way that the human rights topics rights topics can acquire "due status in the curriculum".

Others support the idea that it is preferable to include the human rights contents in every subject, prevading, thus, all school tasks. On the other hand, a third group will argue that it is better to create "learning units in human rights" in order to integrate the contents of different subjects towards the solution of a particular problem. The choice of one or the other possibility will depend upon the educational level as well as the conditions and circumstances under which the curriculum develops. At university level, the subject alternative seems the most appropriate. At the level of elementary education, the inclusion of human rights contents in every subject seems more likely. In secondary education, the creation of problem-solving learning units will probably be more motivating. In this last alternative the contents are organized around a problematic situation in which contradictions are a central element to unveil with a view to the solution of the problem and the fostering of change.

So, for example, if the conflictive situation is "exile", students will be able to identify a number of related problems, such as "the disintegration of the family", "the feeling of alienation", "the status of refugee", etc. Relevant concepts will be defined for each of these problems, as well as related principles and the relationship established with other problems. In this way the problem is clearly outlined and the network of conceptual relationships, activities and behaviour involved are also clarified. Other subjects and disciplines may contribute in this process of clarification of the three learning areas. Thus, in the particular case of "exile", if the problem is that of "alienation", different sciences will make their contribution.

For instance, Psychology, and Sociology will reveal the social and emotional consequences of such a problem; Biology will-relate this situation to that of an organism's rejection of an alien body; History will show the consequences of alienation in some peoples etc. Once the concepts and principles and their relationships with the problem have been defined and clarified, the students will suggest solutions to the problem. For this purpose various methodologies can be applied. The students will then devote themselves to the discussion of the different connotations each of the solutions has. Taking our example again, students could suggest, as a solution, the elimination of frontiers between countries and the creation of a "universal citizenship". The students analyze, discuss and establish the pros and cons of such a solution. Simulation games allow students to check their solutions.

In fact, a list of problematic areas and situations and the problems derived from them could be put down in order to match these areas with those or school contents or subjects which could contribute to the definition, clarification and solution of these problems. In this way, the curriculum is planned around problems concerning human rights and the contents that participate in their solutions are identified. This does not mean that the whole curriculum will be dealing with problematic areas concerning human rights, only that in each school grade it few problems or integrating units will be selected. The Universal Declaration of Human Rights can be the basis of such a list. The participation of teachers and students in the preparation of this list is absolutely essential.

In the next chapter we shall discuss research in human rights—probable fields and other crucial issues of study—wherein researchers can work.

9

RESEARCH IN HUMAN RIGHTS

> "No one will doubt that the legislator should direct his attention above all to the education of youth ... the citizen should be moulded to suit the form of government under which he lives."
>
> —*Aristotle*

First it is pertinent to quote David P. Forsythe and Laurie S. Wiseberg who noted that human rights had become a permanent issue area of world politics. However, very little was known about human rights protection. Thus, they proposed a new research agenda that should be undertaken on the issue Four years later, Jose Zalaquett wrote a report on human rights research published by Columbia University's Center for the Study of Human Rights which determined some research priorities. While most of what Zalaquett defined as prioritary continues to be so today, much scholarly work has already been produced in the last seven years which addresses those issues. Furthermore, human rights researches much more institutionalized than it used to be.

New academic human rights centers have been established in the United States and Europe, and human rights publications are numerous in the Third World today. In short, given that scholars continue to show interest in the subject, it is more difficult to assert subject matters that have received no attention in the recent past. Research on human rights protection and on strategies for the defense of rights has been considerable in late years. This is partly the consequence of the fact that the human rights movement has expanded geographically as well as in membership, developing links to the academic community in every country.

Thus, published books and articles respond. More effectively than in the past to the goals and objectives of activists. Leaders of non-governmental organizations in some countries are aware that university based human rights centers increase the interest for human rights throughout the academic environment. Thus, they support them with enthusiasm. Students and professors are ready to undertake projects which are interesting for NGOs.

Finally, the collapse of Eastern European socialists states, as well as the end of the cold war have strengthened the universal appeal of human rights discourse, leaving partially aside the ideological dispute over human rights approaches that had a relevant impact upon scholarly work. This new context compels us to access recent and current research on human rights, to evaluate existing obstacles to the development and dissemination of these studies, and to propose area studies that should be considered as priority during the coming years.

This paper does not limit itself to the research undertaken in a particular area of the world. However, lack of access to other bibliographical sources has meant an unintended emphasis on studies developed in the United Slates, Canada, Europe, and Latin America. However, that the more general conclusions of this work are also applicable to other regions of the world.

We are focusing on research which is related to the International human rights regime, its norms Institutions, and to the various non-governmental organizations that attend to them. Following partially Zalaquett's work, we have defined the human rights field as comprising the following areas.

- The theoretical foundations of human rights and their relationship to legal, philosophical and religious ideas.
- Standard - setting, interpretation and enforcement of international human rights norms,
- Promotion and implementation of those norms, with special attention given to the strategies used, their impact, as well as the operation of the institutions involved.
- Causes of gross human rights violations and factors that contribute to respect of human rights, as well as description of particular forms of violations.
- The relationship of international human rights to the domestic legal systems, as well as the implementation of these rights in the national legal order.
- The comparison of national human rights protection in the light of the International Bill of Rights.

Given the considerations already made, we have left aside the analysis of national legal and political literature that only deals with domestic constitutional standards with no relation to the international human rights system. Moreover, we are not considering here reports on human rights violations which are basically descriptive and which are prepared by inter governmental bodies or by NGOs.

This does not attempt to evaluate the quality and depth of human rights publications. It simply surveys recent developments in human rights research, noting those areas that have received more attention from the academic community. It describes some of the obstacles facing human rights researchers, specially in the Third World, and it finally evaluates priorities for future research determined on the following basis: either because these subject matters have not been adequately covered or due to the pressing need felt by the human rights community, that certain areas receive more attention.

Recent Research In the Field of Human Rights

The number of regular publications that address human rights issues has rapidly grown in the last ten years. This is certainly the case in the Third World, where new journals have been established as a result of the founding of dynamic NGOs which not only produce reports on present human rights conditions in their countries, but also undertake academic research. Journals created a few years ago have shown considerable stability, which is a signal of the interest in the subject. Moreover, Public International Law. Journals and Political Science Journals regularly include pieces on the subject. Most books written on human rights are comprised of articles written by several authors.

Fewer are the attempts to write comprehensive studies that deal with the normative, as well as the empirical questions involved in the development of the human rights system. While there is nothing wrong with the collection of essays, they certainly lack the coherent and systematic view that results from the writing of a single author. However, some single author, and comprehensive works on human rights have been published in recent years, adding an interesting contribution to the literature on the subject. Another general comment on the literature on human rights, is that it has attracted the interest of legal scholars, philosophers, political scientists, and to a lesser extent, of sociologists. However, very few works have been written by economists, anthropologists and historians. Moreover, human rights is considered to be in the mainstream of law as a discipline. The interest for the subject is lower in the social sciences. In this section, we outline the subject of recent publications in the field of human rights, using its categories the areas that comprise the human rights field and which were defined before.

Theoretical Foundations of International Human Rights

This is an area in which substantial work has already been produced, New additions, specially in the field of legal philosophy have systemized the thoughts and speculations on the subject from eighteenth century theory to modern thought. There are a number of articles on Marxist views on human rights on Christian views on the subject and Theology of Liberation theologians have written on human rights exposing a socialist oriented view.

Most of these writings reflect the Western liberal tradition, as well as the identification of human rights protection with the liberal democratic state. While many authors have argued that the concept of human rights is accepted by all philosophies of our time, a number of authors have argued that internationally recognized human rights are not common to all cultural traditions, nor are they adaptable to a variety of social structures or political regimes.

This debate has possibly opened up to the most fruitful intellectual effort related to different religious and ideological conceptions of human dignity and rights. During recent years conferences and seminars have been organized to address the issue of human rights to cross-cultural perspectives, and books have been written to explore possibilities of cultural reinterpretation and cross-cultural dialogue.

The question of dialogue between the Western liberal tradition and the Chinese one on rights has also been the subject of a recent book on China. Interesting enough, very little has been written on the Latin American cultural tradition on human rights, despite the fact that there are a number of institutes devoted to human rights research in the region. Scholarship on human rights concepts as exposed by different cultural traditions should have an extremely important impact. Debates taking place in the international arena on "new" human rights, such as the right to development, the right to peace, or other collective rights, are probably going to be strongly influenced upon by this theoretical work. The international conjuncture, marked by the crisis of communist regimes, as well as by the end of the cold war, is going to diminish interest on Marxist views on human rights. However, the need to ascertain possibilities for a dialogue among different cultural traditions on rights conceptions, will remain a major subject to interest.

Standard-Setting and Interpretation of Human Rights Norms

This area is the best covered by international lawyers. Most published work so far, deals with the history as well as the obligations contained in the International Bill of Rights, the European Convention on Human Rights and lately, the American Convention on Human Rights. A less covered area, which is receiving much more attention is that of standard setting, specially within the U.N. Also, some articles have been written on procedural steps that should be taken to ensure the seriousness of the process by which the U.N. recognizes new rights. In connection with the same theme, a series of articles have described the evolution and functions of different U.N. human rights bodies The same could he said about some organs of the Inter-American System. It should be noted, however, that these have mainly been legal analyses. With a few exceptions, very little has been written by political scientists on this issue. Most of the traditional civil and political rights have been examined by the literature. Recent articles have dealt with rights that received scant attention in the past. The scholarly debate on "solidarity rights" still goes on. Moreover, there is a new wealth of publications dealing with the fights of special groups, such as indigenous populations, women, and children.

Another area which has experienced considerable development in the recent past is that or the convergence between human rights and humanitarian law. This is due both, to the tireless educational effort or the Red Cross, and to the fact that non-governmental organizations have found that norms of humanitarian law provide a useful legal foundation for their concerns in times of armed conflict. There is still much to be advanced in this area, specially with respect with respect to the assessment of NGO's use of humanitarian law to evaluate rights violations during armed conflict. One aspect which is still lacking in adequate development is that of socio-economic rights. While a few but excellent articles have been written on the subject, the nature of state's obligations is still subject to debate and the question of enforceability of these rights at the national level requires further research.

Implementation of International Human Rights Law

Very few articles have been written on the assessment of the results achieved by human rights bodies in charge of implementing human rights. However, writing on the internal operation of some inter-governmental bodies has steadily increased in the late years. There are still few studies on the comparative effectiveness of different implementation procedures that exist at the universal and regional levels. This is basically due to the fact that interest of social scientists to get involved in such subjects has been scant.

On the other hand, writing on the techniques used by non-governmental organizations to assess compliance with human rights standards by governments has been considerable in the recent past. A number of studies have dealt with the strategies and tactics used by non-governmental organizations to face political repression Fact-finding has been the recurrent theme of numerous articles and of a few books. Foreign policy and its relationship to the national interest, its well its usefulness as a tool for pressing observance of human rights standards continues to be a popular topic for political scientists. However, it still is mainly a concern of American scholars. Very little has been written by nationals from other countries.

Causes of Gross Human Rights Violations and Description of Particular Forms of Violations

Scholarship in this area has considerably increased in recent years. Many authors in the United States, South America and in Europe have written extensively on political repression, its root causes, and evolution. A remarkably interesting development has been the establishment of PIOOM, a Dutch-based Project for the Study of Root Causes of Human Rights Violations, which is encouraging specialists front different parts of the world to undertake research on this subject. Under the auspices of this center, conferences on the monitoring of violations have taken place. This quite interesting development will have a positive effect on scholarship in this area, complementing previous efforts that dealt almost exclusively with the causes of genocide. The description of particular violations such as disappearances and torture were undertaken by Amnesty International a number of years ago. This analysis has been complemented in Latin America with several studies on the psychological consequences of human rights violations.

The Relationship of International Human Rights Law to National Legal Systems

Several articles have been written on the domestic enforcement of international covenants on human rights. Much less has been written on the contrast between national and international legal standards. Another issue area where further work is required deals with the characteristics and functioning of domestic state institutions in charge of applying international human rights law within each country. The existing mechanisms for implementing rights obligations in the socio-economic field at the domestic level remain as a subject which has attracted very little attention from academics. Comprehensive analyses about internal legislation enacted by different countries to enforce certain human rights treaties is also lacking. A subject that has received considerable attention is that of the policies of democratic regimes towards past human rights violations, in the light of international law. A number of articles and reports by Americas Watch and Amnesty International have dealt with the prosecution of human rights violators in Argentina and in Uruguay after civilian authorities took office. The legality of amnesties and pardons in such circumstances have been analyzed in detail.

The Comparison of National Human Rights Systems in the Light of International Human Rights Law

A few articles, books and conferences have been devoted to this issue, analyzing different legal traditions and their

means that new publications are mailed as a gift to a few persons in each country, but they fail to reach most potential readers. Human rights publications in Europe and North America are extremely expensive for Third World standards, which necessarily means that human rights scholars lack access to the latest developments an their field.

Discussion on these limitations is important, to encourage private or public foundations to get interested in supporting academic research and university teaching on human rights. However, it is realistic to expect that funding for activism and advocacy continues to be a priority. Their short-term results in terms of achieving a better protection of rights are certainly far greater than those that could be obtained by a better and more analytical academic research. Academic researchers working on human rights should strengthen their contacts and engage in a fruitful dialogue with NGOs. While such contacts exist in many countries, more is needed to dissipate mutual misunderstandings. In fact, good theoretical work on human rights is positive for scholarship and for activism.

Collaboration between the two groups might facilitate fund raising and provoke greater attention for Third World scholarship abroad. Some of the problems we have touched upon, are not exclusive to the Third World. To a much lesser extent they are also present in rich democratic societies. Philip Alston, writing on deficiencies of existing academic approaches to International Human Rights Law, has said:

> "International human rights scholarship is essentially defensive as a result of preoccupation with short-term results which are sometimes achieved at the expense of long-term coherence. The scholarship is, for the most part, narrowly focused in terms of the issues with which it is concerned, and for that reason has tended

to attract a caste of academic exponents whose vision and range of concerns is limited".

As Alston explains, the reasons for these shortcomings are to be found in the unavoidable tension between the need to prescribe and make recommendation to face urgent situations and the requirement to consolidate the theoretical foundations of scholarship. In the field of human rights, where urgent situation are the rule, it is quite difficult to avoid this tension. One of its consequences, though, is that mainstream academics are reluctant to engage in human rights research. Moreover, the highly normative character of the subject discourages economists and other social scientists to relate human rights to the major interests of their disciplines. These obstacles are cited to explain some of the deficiencies of current scholarship, as well as the difficulties faced by human rights scholars. It is feasible that lack of development of human rights research will continue to be the rule in some disciplines. On the other hand, our description of recent publications on the subject shows that interest for it has increased in recent years, and that many publications have filled research needs that existed ten years ago. The first two parts of this paper pointed to the many needs that still exist in the field of human rights research. The next one lists research needs and priorities that result from the previous survey. The agenda reflects as it is obvious, perceptions of existing theoretical needs, as well as those required for the promotion of human rights.

Needs and Priorities for Further Research

The topics listed as priority are organized under the following headings: theoretical foundations of human rights, as well as historical development of this ideal; interpretation and definition of international human rights; promotion and implementation of those rights, including tactics and techniques used by different institutions and actors; causes of gross human rights violations; comparison of national rights systems.

Theoretical Foundations of Human Rights As Well As Historical Development of this Idea

As we said earlier, there are a good number of publications on theoretical foundations of human rights. However, there are very few historical studies that cover the field. The following is a sample of subjects which require further research and which are priorities.

a) The universality of human rights.
   - Basis for a Cross-cultural dialogue on human rights perceptions.
   - Comparative Perceptions of Human Dignity Held by Differ Religions and Cultures.
   - Anthropological Studies on the development of human rights conceptions in different cultures.
   - The conflict between individual and group rights. This conflict expresses itself in various areas such as the rights of indigenous populations, rights of peoples and others.

b) The Development of Human Rights Conceptions,
   - Historical development of ideas of freedom and equality in different regions such as Latin America and Africa.
   - History of non-violent movements that have defended human rights.
   - The history of the evolution of different institutions in charge of protecting rights in different countries. We are thinking here on the historical development of the role of judicial

institutions, and legislative control of the executive branch, specially during times of crisis.

Interpretation and Definition of International Human Rights Law

a) • Collective Rights

- The right to self-determination and the situation of ethnic minorities.
- The Right to Development in the Context of the Present Economic and monetary system. Is it feasible?
- The Right to Environment in the Context of North-South Relations,

b) Civil and Political Rights.

- Comparative Interpretation of these Rights by Regional Courts and Commissions.
- Religious Freedom. Are there permissible limits to certain religious practices advocated by sects whose proselytizing techniques might violate freedom of conscience?
- Compatibility of the Right to a Fair Trial and Inquisitive Criminal Procedures.
- Analysis of limitations Imposed on the Enjoyment of these Rights and Based on Considerations of National Security, Public Morals, and Public Order. What is the Range of Discretion that Governments Possess to Limit the Exercise of Rights Based on these Grounds?
- What are the existing tensions between the principle of equal protection and measures aimed at solving the problems of special groups or minorities?

c) Economic, Social and Cultural Rights.
   - The right to health care and its protection in different societies.
   - Protection of minoritarian cultural views. Applicable internal legislation.
   - Principles for monitoring compliance with socio-economic and cultural standards.
   - Studies on the Domestic Machinery in charge of Enforcing Socio- Economic standards.

Promotion and Implementation of Human Rights Standards

- Comparative Human Rights Educational Policies in different societies.
- Human Rights Education Programs for different age groups. Evaluation of their impact.
- Assessment of the comparative effectiveness of different procedures used by inter-governmental organizations to monitor compliance with human rights standards.
- Historical studies on the politics of certain intergovernmental bodies, such as the Inter-American Commission, or the United Nations Human Rights Commission. Most studies done with this regard have been international legal analyses, rather than social science studies,
- Analysis of the implications of the end of the Cold War for the evolution and change of the United Nation's role In the human rights field.
- Comparison of foreign policy towards human rights issues taken by different countries.
- Empirical evaluation of the impact of economic and diplomatic sanctions imposed by governments or

intergovernmental organizations on the observance of human rights.

- Comparative studies of national human rights movements, their relationship to political parties and social forces, and their strategies and tactics.

Causes of Human Rights Violations

- Studies of the different forms assumed by gross human rights violations: mass killings disappearances, selective murder, political trial.
- Political, ideological and economic factors which create conditions for the massive violations of human rights,
- Comparative case studies on Ethnic conflicts,
- Case studies on conflict .resolution measures after processes of internal armed conflicts that have resulted in gross human rights and humanitarian law violations.
- Analyses of police training and its effect upon the enjoyment of human rights.
- Relationship between types of economic policies and levels of political repression.

Comparison of National Rights Systems

There are many possible approaches to this type of research. It could be done comparing national legislative approaches to the protection of certain rights, such as the right to life, or the right to privacy. An important contribution would be the analysis of comparative policies towards implementing international labor standards, Another aspect that deserves attention is that of anti-discrimination policies, on grounds of sex, religion or race. Another approach would be to undertake the comparative study of Institutions which play an important role in protecting human rights, such as legislatures, the judicial branch, and other public, but independent commissions, such as human rights commissions.

A consideration of their traditions, as well as their actions in the protection of rights would be desirable. Many more topics could be added to the aforementioned list of themes considered to be a priority for researchers. Moreover, research on more traditional topic, has certainly not been exhausted. Just a few recommendations are in order here to improve communication among researchers, and to strengthen the quality of the research that is being done.

First, the quality of research, as well as its influence in shaping the political agenda depends on the establishment of new research and academic centers, specially if linked to universities. It is urgent that these centers attract the interest of economists, anthropologists and development experts. To achieve this result, they should undertake inter-disciplinary research and organize conferences that deal with topics that are related to the major interests in some disciplines.

Second, dissemination of human rights research should be emphasized. In some regions, such as Latin America, the founding of editorial companies that distribute this literature would be useful.

Another alternative, is to subsidize distribution of human rights publications by existing companies.

Third, most academic events dealing with human rights take place in the First World. Attendance by Third World scholars is not as high as it should be. Cross-fertilization among scholars of different regions of the 'Third World should be encouraged. We are certainly aware that the costs involved in such widely attended meetings are extremely high. Nevertheless, this is a goal we should keep in mind. Fourth, the expansion of university teaching programs, specially in the Third World, requires a major effort consisting of the publication and dissemination of teaching materials as widely as possible.

Social Science Research in Support of Human Rights

What kinds of people express support for civil liberties and human rights and what kinds of people oppose them? Why do some people give verbal support to the abstract principle of civil liberties for everyone and, at the same time, advocate destroying the rights of their fellow citizens? What structural factors in a nation or community encourage and sustain civil liberties and human rights? A growing body of studies conducted in North America, in some western European countries, and elsewhere has explored these questions. Research results are discussed in this chapter, and a model is developed in an attempt to explain the social bases of support for human rights.

In this review essay, the behavioral approach, to social research is emphasized. David Danelski summarizes the use of a behavioral approach to human rights: One of the more fruitful aspects of a behavioral conception of human rights is that it can be used in scientific research. Each of the component behaviors of human rights can be specified empirically, and survey-research methods can be used for that purpose.

World wide inventories of man's perceptions of man, of his acknowledgements of the kind of treatment man is entitled to as man, and of rights in action would be a beginning. A comparative study of man's differing acknowledgements would be as revealing as would a comparison of acknowledgements and rights in action. With such data, men's perceptions of other men could be explored more fully and profoundly than they have ever been before, and hypotheses concerning man's failure to perceive some of his fellow men as fully human could be tested. The whole acknowledgement process could be explored in terms of learning theory and other psychological theories. And finally hypotheses could be tested concerning the conditions under which they do not.

These cursory comments about possible research paths in regard to the study of human rights are at best suggestive. The only point being made here is that once human rights are defined in terms of observable behavior, such research can be carried on. In this essay, only the behavioral approach to civil liberties is considered, but it is recognized that the sociology of civil liberties and the political philosophy of civil liberties are, in the words of W.G. Runciman, "inextricably linked." Behaviorism predicts the probable outcome of actions, but it does not tell us which actions to take. It is important to ask how men do behave, as well as how they ought to behave.

There is much documentary literature on the legal basis of human rights, on the historical development of civil liberties and human rights in specific countries, on specific court decisions, on the role of the United Nations in the area of human rights, and on the relationship of political philosophy and human rights. There is less information on organizations (other than courts) which may protect or impede the protection of specific human rights.

Problems of Survey Research

There are very few international comparative studies of

attitudes and opinions in the field of human rights that cover various population segments (that is, social classes, religious groups). There is also a lack of consensus among social scientists as to what methodological approach should be taken in comparative research. Gabriel Almond and Sidney Verba's study of the political cultures of five nations is widely viewed as a model of comparative analysis using survey research techniques. Almond and Verba sampled household in the United States, Mexico, Italy, Germany, and Great Britain. Employing the concept of "political culture," they inquired into the political orientation of citizens of these five nations. Their research is developed in terms of

(1) cognitive orientation, or the "knowledge of and belief about the political system, its roles and incumbents of these roles, its inputs and its' outputs";
(2) affective orientation, or "feelings about the political system, its roles, personnel, and performance"; and
(3) evaluational orientation, or "the judgments and opinions about political objects that typically involve the combination of value standards and criteria with information and feelings."

Almond and Verba apply the methods of systematic survey research to the study of comparative politics, and they acknowledge the influence of voting studies on their procedures. They note the great expense, labor, advance planning, coordination, and substantial risks involved in cross-national surveys and, at the same time list several of their advantages.

First, "a direct look at political attitudes ... is useful in order to validate the inferences we have made about them from other material, and to develop independent measures that can be used to explain other phenomena."

A second advantage is that quantitative meaning can be given to typically vague analytical terms such as "characteristic" of country A or the "usual" attitude of workers in country B. Comparative analysis of answers to the same question can show variations within and between nations.

Third, for the comparative analysis of political behavior, the use of crossnational surveys seems quite apt, because "the statistical methods by which one analyses the results of survey research are essentially comparative."

A fourth advantage of cross-national surveys is that one must undertake "a very important task for comparative analysis: the development of a means of conceptualizing politics in ways that have wide applicability." The .scarcity of effective comparative opinion research is understandable in view of the large costs involved. Thus, when crossnational surveys or, in particular, panel surveys, are too expensive or difficult, the researcher may utilize polls conducted for different purposes based on different types of samples in several countries.

This is the approach of Seymour Martin Lipset in his analysis of "working class authoritarianism," which utilizes a secondary analysis of opinion data from several western European countries, and from Mexico, Japan, and the United States. Pursuit of comparative research may involve not only financial cost but also some political risk. Some regimes, such as those in Spain and the Soviet Union, forbid social research which may reveal dissatisfaction or revisionist attitudes among their citizens.

Both crossnational surveys and comparative analyses of polls taken in different countries are few in number. Research interest in civil liberties or human rights is a reflection of preoccupations or restraints on social scientists during certain periods in the history of a given country. In the United States, for example, some social scientists during the 1950s felt personally threatened by the attack of government agents on their civil rights. Still, important research on civil liberties was undertaken at that time.

Survey research faces other practical obstacles. It may prove abortive as the investigator comes to appreciate the effect of political culture on his own research design. For example, political controversy, which in the United States may be phrased in terms of battles over human rights, may be phrased in other countries in terms of class warfare, class rivalry, of some other referrent. Absence of research models further explains the scarcity of cumulative research on support for civil liberties.

Among the social surveys utilizing nationwide samples concerning attitudes toward civil liberties, Samuel Stouffer's Communism, Conformity, and Civil Liberties is preeminent in the literature. In the spring of 1954, over six thousand respondents were polled by two of the foremost public opinion research organizations in the United States. Topics covered in this survey included: What are the attitudes of civic leaders as compared with the rank and file within a community? Do attitudes towards civil liberties differ in different regions of the country? When urban areas are compared with rural areas? Among men as compared with women? What role does religion play? How important are agencies of mass communications? What can be accomplished by responsible citizens in their local communities?

This survey pioneered the effective use of so called "free answer" or "open-ended" questions, in which the respondent answers questions in his own words rather than in terms of a precoded set of responses. Furthermore, a series of questions is asked rather than relying on a single question to summarize a given opinion. Stouffer tied his research to previous surveys on the subject and many later researchers profitably followed his example of pursuing cumulative research strategies.

Problems of Conceptualizing Human Rights

Attempts to provide nominal and operational definitions of rights and freedoms have a long history. The doctrine of "natural rights" or "the rights of man" was codified in writings of eighteenth century philosophers. The documents of the American Revolution, including the Declaration of Independence and the Bill of Rights, along with the French Declaration of the Rights of Man of 1789, are of particular importance in the history of human rights, for they stated in formal terms the universal conception of rights-that all men have rights vis-a-vis the government of a state.

It remains to be seen whether the United Nations Universal Declaration of Human Rights of 1948 will be equally important in the development of the concepts of human rights. Recently, there has been expansion of the scope of topics considered under the heading of human rights. In an anthology honoring the fiftieth anniversary of the American Civil Liberties Union, separate chapters are devoted to a long list of rights never explicitly mentioned in eighteenth century documents. They include equal educational opportunity, equal employment, housing, welfare, legal services, suffrage, participation in politics, protest, free association, publishing, access to mass media, property, religious liberty, control of the use of one's body, and travel.

This list is by no means complete, however, especially for industrialized countries with democratic forms of government. For example, the right to decent environmental quality and the right to privacy are omitted, yet court cases and legislation designed to protect these rights are rapidly developing, a least in the United States and Canada.

Even when identified and guaranteed by laws, constitutions, or creeds, and', reaffirmed by court decisions in test cases, rights (which often conflict with one' another) are difficult to define in actual practice and more difficult to implement. The articulation of human rights on a worldwide basis has barely begun. The 1948 United Nations declaration is not universally accepted by member nations as a program of rights, and even those rights upon which there is wide constitutional consensus are not universally implemented. For systematic comparative analysis, a careful conceptualization of rights needs to be undertaken.

Consistent with usage throughout this volume, the distinction is between civil liberties, civil rights, and human rights. Civil liberties refers to rights of persons vis-a-vis government. These include freedom of speech, freedom of association and assembly, freedom of religion, rights of conscience, and rights to due process under law, Civil rights in the United States is identified with the struggles of blacks and other ethnic minorities for equal participation in the political and social life of the country.

In early writings (before 1960) and in some comparative work, civil liberties and civil rights are used interchangeably. Human rights refers broadly to civil rights and to civil liberties but also to a wide range of emerging rights that include housing, jobs, and health services. Conceptual definition has its corollary in the area of operational definition. Various social researchers have used a wide variety of operational definitions and different indices or scales, to define the abstract concepts of human rights. Gerhard Lenski

reemphasized: opinions are formed and behavior occurs within the context of a political culture. Cross-national comparison of attitudes has meaning only if the social scientist conceptualizes his study within an international framework. Moreover, the international framework must include a time orientation. Most of the surveys cited are admittedly time-bound as well as culture-bound. They are conducted at a specific time and place, and any attempt to use the data in a developmental model is fraught with methodological difficulties. The studies reflect the controversies of the period in which the data were collected, as well as the cultural biases of the respondents at a particular time.

In America, for example, there was at certain periods an almost paranoid concern with the threat of communism; in the 1950s, Americans were most unwilling to guarantee freedom of speech, assembly, due process, or the right to publish, to anyone labeled "communist" or "Communist sympathizer." Frede Castberg describes similar problems in France and Germany. In both of these countries, heated debates occurred and bills were introduced in the legislatures to exclude the Communist Party, as an enemy of freedom, from the constitutional protection of free speech and freedom of association. Polls reflect a climate of opinion, but long-term trends are rarely tapped by national polls, and research on cross-cultural trends has barely begun.

Because polling was developed as a methodology in the United States in the 1930s, some studies of trends do exist. Herbert Hyman and Paul Sheatsley find that in America, beginning in 1937, when the first Gallup polls were conducted, and through World War II and the Cold War until about 1950, support for restrictions on freedom of speech, assembly, and academic freedom was increasing. In a review of polls concerning freedom of the press, Hazel Erskine finds tentative evidence that few Americans would accord complete freedom of speech to political extremists, and that permissiveness towards radicals has been decreasing in the United States since the 1930s. Comparative studies of support for human rights cannot ignore the bias which was created by feelings and beliefs during certain historical periods.

A further pitfall of survey research is the assumption that all opinions of all persons are equal to one another. The intensity with which a person holds a belief or opinion and the clarity with which persons perceive issues vary greatly. Education and other social factors, along with individual intelligence and personal life experiences, mold opinion. When both citizen A and citizen B say that they oppose granting voting rights to eighteen-year-olds, A may express stronger ideological opposition than B. Of course, A and B may also vary greatly in their ability to act upon their beliefs. That is why a comparison of community leaders and followers is important. Community leaders have more power and resources to implement human rights than do followers; at the same time they will be somewhat sensitive to their opinions.

There is also considerable controversy over the relation between attitudes and behavior. It would be naive to assume there is always a one-to-one correlation between opinions and behavior in a real situation. It is difficult, however, to discern the effects of attitudes, opinions, and situational factors on behavior. Whereas it is frequently said that changing attitudes lead to changing behavior, the reverse may also be true. Thomas Pettigrew makes the point that changing behavior which leads to changing attitudes may be, in fact, more common. He writes: "After the fact, individuals modify their ideas to fit their new act, often proving amazingly adaptable in doing so. Indeed, considerable research suggests that this behavior-to-attitude cycle of change is generally easier and more effective than the attitude-to-behavior 'cycle." Too much reliance must not be placed on cross-sectional studies in attempting to understand the development of attitudes towards human rights.

There is, for example, a great deficiency of panel or other longitudinal studies which employ the same sample of people to see how or whether or not opinions change over time. In nearly all the cross-sectional surveys, persons over fifty years of age are much less tolerant of political deviants than are people under thirty. What is the effect of aging on political opinions when aging is separated from the effects of education, religion, and social class? Do generations share similar experiences which mold attitudes, although they develop different attitudes towards human rights? These are the types of intriguing questions about which there is as yet little information. Clearly, where the topic of survey research is complex, the methodology is correspondingly complicated. Cross-national research on human rights is also made complex by the historical dimension of time. An historicist might argue that the unique rights developed in each separate nation defy efforts to generalize about historical processes among nations. But people do make decisions under certain historical circumstances, and it is possible to identify factors which are conducive to the development of human rights. People are not robots in history, but neither are they free from the influences of history and circumstances. Lipset, in analyzing the development and maintenance of two-party democracy in labor unions, discusses factors which resulted in a "favorable throw of the die," making it more likely that in the future a two-party system would be maintained.

Therefore researchers who study support for the principles of human rights must deal with a number of complex, interacting variables. They include: (1) changing definitions of human rights and shifting priorities of rights during different periods in history; (2) the relation between attitudes verbally expressed by individuals and their actual behavior in specific social situations; (3) the reliability and validity of scales and indices of attitudes used in cross-national surveys; and (4) the specific historical conditions affecting such research factors as the possible fear of respondents in answering questions.

APPENDIX

ACADEMIC DEGREES IN HUMAN RIGHTS EDUCATIONS

Continent	*Country*	*University*	*Coursename*	*Type of course*	*Duration of course*
Not Applicable	Distance	Oxford University	Master's Degree in International Human Rights Law	MA	24 months
Not Applicable	UK	The London School of Economics and Political Science	Ms Human Rights	Other Masters	12 months
Africa	Egypt	American University in Cairo	Migration and Refugee Studies	MA	24 months
Africa	Egypt	American University	MA International Human Rights Law	MA	24 months
Africa	Egypt	American University	Graduate Diploma in Forced Migration and Refugee Studies	Diploma	12 months
Africa	Ghana	University of Education, Winneba	Human Rights	MA	12 months
Africa	South Africa	University Pretoria	LL.M. in Human Rights & Constitutional Practice	LL.M.	12 months

Africa	South Africa	University Pretoria	LL.M. in Human Rights and Democratisation in Africa	LL.M.	12 months
Africa	Uganda	Makerere University	Human Rights	MA	24 months
Americas	America	denver University	Human Rights	MA	24 months
Americas	Canada	Mcgill University	Human Rights and Cultural Diversity	LL.M.	18 months
Americas	Colombia	Universidad del Externado (Colombia), Universidad Carlos III de Madrid	Master en Derechos Humanos y Democratizacion	MA	12 months
Americas	Costa Rica	Universidad Estatal a Distancia (UNED)	Maestria Profesional en Derechos Humanos (Master in Human Rights)	Other Masters	12 months
Americas	Costa Rica	Peace University	Master's Degree in International Law and Human Rights	Other Masters	12 months
Americas	Guatemala	Universidad de San Carlos	Master of Human Rights	MA	12 months
Americas	Mexico	FLACSO	MaestrÃ-a en Derechos Humanos y Democracia	Other Masters	19 months
Americas	United States	Arizona State University at the West Campus	MA in Social Justice and Human Rights	MA	18 months
Americas	USA	Emory University	Graduate certificate in Human Rights	Certificate	12 months
Americas	USA	John Jay College of Criminal Justice	International Crime and Justice	MA	24 months
Americas	USA	Yale, MacMillan Center	MA in International Relations (concentration human rights)	MA	24 months

contd...

Continent	Country	University	Coursename	Type of course	Duration of course
Americas 12 months	USA	St Thomas University	LL.M. Program in	Human Rights	LL.M.
		School of Law, Miami	Intercultural		
Americas	USA	School of International Training, Vermont	MA in Conflict Transfor mation	MA	12 months
Americas	USA	University of Massachussets, Amherst	MA in Social Justice Education	M.Ed.	24 months
Americas	USA	Harvard Law School	Master of Laws	LL.M.	24 months
Americas	USA	Georgetown Law	Master of Laws	LL.M.	12 months
Americas	USA	Indiana School of Law	LL.M. in International Human Rights Law	LL.M.	12 months
Americas	USA	Notre Dame Law School, Indiana	LL.M. in International Human Rights Law	LL.M.	12 months
Americas	USA	Fletcher School, Tufts University	Master of Arts For Mid-Care er Professionals	MA	12 months
Americas	USA	Fletcher School, Tufts University	Master of Arts in Law and Diplomacy (MALD)	MA	24 months
Americas	USA	University of Denver, Josef Korbel School of International Studies	MA in International Human Rights	MA	24 months
Americas	USA	Columbia, School of International Public Affairs	Masters in International Affairs	MA	24 months

Americas	USA	NYU School of Law	Master of Laws	LL.M.	12 months
Americas	USA	Northwestern University School of Law	LLM Concentration in International Human Rights	LL.M.	12 months
Americas	USA	Notre Dame Law School, Indiana	J.S.D. (doctorate) in International Human Rights Law	LL.D. (J.S.D)	12 months
Americas	USA	American University, Washington College of Law	MA in International Human Rights	MA	12 months
Americas	USA	Columbia Law School	LL.M.	LL.M.	12 months
Americas	USA	Columbia, Graduate School of Arts and Sciences	Liberal Studies Masters in Human Rights Studies	MA	24 months
Asia	China	Hong Kong	Master of Laws in Human Rights	LL.M.	12 months
Asia	India	IIHR	PGDHR(Human Rights)	Other Masters	24 months
Asia	INDIA	Panjab University Chandigarh	Master in Human Right & Duties	MA	24 months
Asia	India	Indian Law Society	International Diploma in international diploma in mental health law and human rights	MA	12 months
Asia	India	Indian Society for International Law, New Delhi	Human Rights, Humanitarian and Refugee Law	Diploma	12 months
Asia	Nepal	Kathmandu School of Law	MA in Conflict and International Humanitarian Laws	MA	12 months
Asia	Nepal	Kathmandu School of Law	MA in Human Rights	MA	12 months
Asia	Nepal	Kathmandu School of Law	LL.M. in Human Rights and Gender Justice	LL.M.	12 months

contd...

Continent	*Country*	*University*	*Coursename*	*Type of course*	*Duration of course*
Asia	Thailand	Mahidol	International Masters of Human Rights and Social Development	Other Masters	12 months
Asia	Thailand	Mahidol	PhD (Human Rights and Peace)	MA	36 months
Europe	Austria	Donau-UniversitÃ£t Krems	Menschenrechte / Human Rights	MA	24 months
Europe	Finland	Abo Akademi Institute for Human Rights	Masters in International Human Rights Law	LL.M.	24 months
Europe	France	UniversitÃ© de Caen Basse-Normandie	Master 2 Droit public et Droits fondamentaux	MA	12 months
Europe	Germany	European University Viadrina Frankfurt (Oder)	Master of International Human Rights and Humanitarian Law	LL.M.	18 months
Europe	Hungary	Central European University	Master of Laws in Human Rights	LL.M.	12 months
Europe	Hungary	Central European University	Master of Arts in Human Rights	MA	12 months
Europe	Ireland	National University of Ireland, Galway	International Human Rights Law	PhD	36 months
Europe	Ireland	Dublin	MSc Human Rights	Other Masters	12 months
Europe	Ireland	Galway	LL.M. in International Human Rights Law	LL.M.	12 months
Europe	Italy	University of Bologna	Master in Human Rights and Humanitarian Intervention	Other Masters	15 months
Europe	Italy	Scuola Superiore Santâ€™ Anna	Master in Human Rights and Conflict Management	MA	12 months
Europe	Malta	University Malta	Mediterranean Master's Programme in Human Rights and Democratisation	Other Masters	12 months

Europe	Multiple	Seven universities in Belgium, France, Germany, Ireland, Spain, Sweden, Netherlands	Master in International Humanitarian Action	MA	16 months
Europe	Multiple	European Inter-University Centre for Human Rights and Democratisation	European Master's Programme in Human Rights and Democratisation	Other Masters	12 months
Europe	Netherlands	Utrecht	LL.M. International and European Protection of Human Rights	LL.M.	12 months
Europe	Netherlands	Utrecht	MA Conflict Studies and Human Rights	MA	12 months
Europe	Norway	Oslo	Master of Philosophy in the Theory and Practice of Human Rights	Other Masters	24 months
Europe	Spain	Instituto de Derechos Humanos, Universidad Carlos III de Madrid	Postgrado en Estudios Avanzados en Derechos Humanos	PhD	24 months
Europe	Spain	Instituto de Derechos Humanos, Universidad Carlos III de Madrid	Master en Derechos Fundamentales	MA	12 months
Europe	Spain	Deusto University, Pedro Arrupe Human Rights Institute	Migration and Conflicts in a Global Society	MA	12 months
Europe	Sweden	Lund	LL.M. in International Human Rights Law	LL.M.	12 months
Europe	Switzerland	Geneva	Master of Advanced Studies in Humanitarian Action	Other Masters	12 months
Europe	Switzerland	Institut Universitaire Kurt Bosch, Sion	Master of Advanced Studies in Children's Rights (MCR)	LL.M.	12 months
Europe	Switzerland	CUDIH Geneva	Master in Advanced Studies in IHL	LL.M.	12 months

contd...

Continent	Country	University	Coursename	Type of course	Duration of course
Europe	Turkey	Maltepe University	M.A. Human Rights	MA	22 months
Europe	Turkey	Bilgi University	Human Rights Law	LL.M.	24 months
Europe	UK	School of Advanced Study, University of London - Institute of Commonwealth Studies	Human Rights	PhD	36 months
Europe	UK	York	LLM in International Human Rights Law and Practice	LL.M.	12 months
Europe	UK	University of Ulster	LLM Human Rights Law and Transitional Justice	LL.M.	12 months
Europe	UK	City University	MA Refugee Studies	MA	12 months
Europe	UK	Roehampton University	MA/PGDip/PGCert Human Rights and International Relations	MA	10 months
Europe	UK	University of Ulster	LLM Human Rights law	LL.M.	12 months
Europe	UK	City University	MA International Politics and Human Rights	MA	12 months
Europe	UK	School of Advanced Study, University of London - Institute for the Study of the Americas	Human Rights	PhD	36 months
Europe	UK	York	Applied Human Rights	MA	12 months
Europe	UK	University of Sussex	MA Human Rights	MA	12 months
Europe	UK	Kent	MA in Human Rights	MA	12 months

Europe	UK	Oxford	Masters in International Human Rights Law (part time)	Other Masters	24 months
Europe	UK	Coventry	International Law & Human Rights	LL.M.	12 months
Europe	UK	City University London	LL.M. International Human Rights Law	LL.M.	12 months
Europe	UK	Edinburgh University	LL.M. in European and International Human Rights Law	12 months LL.M.	
Europe	UK	City University London	MA in Human Rights	MA	12 months
Europe	UK	Brunel	International Human Rights Law LL.M. and Diploma	LL.M.	12 months
Europe	UK	Bristol	The International Human Rights	LL.M.	12 months
Europe	UK	UCE Birmingham	LL.M. in International Human Rights	Other Masters	12 months
Europe	UK	Birmingham	Masters in Human Rights and Human Values	Other Masters	12 months
Europe	UK	Birkbeck	Human Rights (MA / LL.M.)	Other Masters	12 months
Europe	UK	Belfast University	LL.M. in Human Rights Law	LL.M.	12 months
Europe	UK	Belfast University	LL.M./MSSc in Human Rights and Criminal Justice	Other Masters	12 months
Europe	UK	Aberdeen	LL.M. in Human Rights and Criminal Justice	LL.M.	12 months
Europe	UK	Aberdeen	LL.M. Human Rights	LL.M.	12 months
Europe	UK	Coventry	Human Rights &/or Criminal	LL.M.	12 months

contd...

Continent	Country	University	Coursename	Type of course	Duration of course
			Justice		
Europe	UK	Coventry	Human Rights &/or Criminal Justice	LL.M.	12 months
Europe	UK	Kingston	MA Human Rights	MA	12 months
Europe	UK	Kent	MA in Public International Law	MA	12 months
Europe	UK	Keele	Masters Human Rights, Globalisation and Justice	Other Masters	12 months
Europe	UK	Keele	Masters Gender, Sexuality & Human Rights	Other Masters	12 months
Europe	UK	School of Advanced Study, University of London - Institute of Commonwealth Studies	Understanding and Securing Human Rights	MA	12 months
Europe	UK	Hull	LL.M. in International Human Rights Law	LL.M.	12 months
Europe	UK	Hull	LL.M. in Human Rights and Criminology	LL.M.	12 months
Europe	UK	Glascow	LL.M. Human Rights Law	Other Masters	12 months
Europe	UK	Essex	Health Care Law and Human Rights	LL.M.	12 months
Europe	UK	Essex	LL.M. International Human Rights Law	LL.M.	12 months

Europe	**UK**	**Essex**	Theory and Practice of Human Rights	MA	12 months
Europe	UK	Glascow	MSc Human Rights & International Politics	Other Masters	12 months
Europe	UK	Glascow	LL.M. and Postgraduate Diploma in Human Rights Law	Other Masters	12 months
Europe	United Kingdom	University of Essex	International Human Rights Law and Humanitarian Law	LL.M.	12 months
Europe	United Kingdom	Middlesex University	MA Human Rights and Business	MA	24 months
Oceania	Australia	University of Sydney	Master of Human Rights	MA	12 months
Oceania	Australia	Monash	Master of Laws (Human Rights)	LL.M.	12 months
Oceania	Australia	Centre for Human Rights Education, Curtin University	Masters of Human Rights Practice	MA	18 months
Oceania	Australia	Centre for Human Rights Education, Curtin University	Masters of Human Rights Education	MA	18 months

sovereignty over territory and people outside its own boundaries in order to facilitate domination over natural resources, labor, and markets. The term also refers to a set of beliefs used to legitimize or promote this system, especially the belief that the mores of the colonizer are superior to those of the colonized.

Community – A group of people who identify with each other, have common interests, or are viewed as forming a distinct segment of society. The word community can also mean a society as a whole. A Human Rights Communityis a community based on human rights, where respect for the fundamental dignity of each individual is recognized as essential to society.

Community Service – Service that is designed to assist in addressing community problems such as housing, poverty, government, recreation, employment, youth opportunities, transportation, health, and land use.

Conflict Resolution – Reconciling opposing perspectives, stories, or experiences and deciding on a response that promotes and protects the human rights of all parties concerned.

Convention –A legally binding agreement between nations designed to protect human rights (used interchangeably with *treaty* and *covenant*). *Conventions* are considered to have more legal force than *declarations* because governments are legally bound to enforce the agreements that they have ratified. When the *UN General Assembly* adopts a *convention,* it creates international standards for action and behavior. Once a *convention* is adopted by the *UNGeneral Assembly, Member States* can then ratify it, thereby promising to uphold it. Governments that violate the standards set forth in a *convention* can then be censured by the UN and by governments.

Convention on the Elimination of all Forms of Discrimination Against Women (CEDAW or Women's Convention; adopted 1979, entered into force 1981) – The most comprehensive legally binding international *convention* prohibiting discrimination against women and obligating governments to take affirmative steps to advance the equality of women.

Convention on the Rights of the Child – (Children's Convention; adopted 1989, entered into force 1990) – *Convention* setting forth a full spectrum of civil, cultural, economic, social, and political rights for children.

Covenant – A legally binding agreement between nations (used synonymously with *convention* and *treaty*). The major international human rights *covenants*, both adopted in 1966 (and entered into force in 1976), are the International Covenant on Civil and Political Rights (ICCPR) and the International Covenant on Economic, Social and Cultural Rights (ICESCR).

Creed – A set of fundamental beliefs or guiding principles. A creed can be either religious or secular.

Critical Thinking – Analyzing and contemplating past and present experiences, as well as future possibilities, by taking into account multiple perspectives on a story or narrative..

Critically Analyzing History – Analyzing a historical event or era from different cultural perspectives, including birth, gender, language, national or social origin, political or other opinion, property, or other status..

Cultural Rights – The right to preserve and develop one's cultural identity, as well as the right to protect endangered cultures.

Customary International Law – Law that becomes binding

on nations through general acceptance as a matter of legal obligation. When enough states have begun to behave as though some principle is law, it becomes law "by use"; this is one of the main sources of international law.

Cynicism (Opposite: Optimism) – An attitude of scornful or jaded negativity, especially a general distrust of the integrity or professed motives of others.

Declaration – A document comprising standards that nations agree upon, but which are not legally binding like treaty provisions. UN conferences, such as the 1993 UN Conference on Human Rights in Vienna and the 1995 World Conference for Women in Beijing, usually produce two sets of declarations: one written by government representatives and one written by *Nongovernmental Organizations* (*NGOs*). The *UN General Assembly* often issues influential declarations.

Democracy – A system of government in which people's views are reflected and the right of political participation is guaranteed. Such a form of government involves the principles of promoting and protecting human rights, social equality, and respect for the individual within a community.

Direct Action – Those tactics that can be undertaken by people themselves, without the help of government agencies, lawyers, or other institutions. Examples include picketing, work slowdowns, strikes, occupation of buildings, and marches.

Discrimination (Opposite: Non-Discrimination) – Distinction between individuals not based on legitimate terms; arbitrary bias for or against an individual or a group that fails to take true account of their characteristics or treat an individual or a group in a just and equitable manner. Discrimination can be based on age, birth, color, creed, disability, ethnic origin, familial status, gender, language, marital status, political or other opinion, public assistance, race, religion or belief, sex, or sexual orientation.

Distinguishing Between Fact, Opinion, and Reasoned Judgment – *Fact* can be defined as knowledge or information based on real occurrences or empirical evidence, while *opinions* are beliefs or conclusions held with confidence but not substantiated by positive knowledge or proof. Judgment means discernment, assessment and/or comparison of ideas to arrive at a conclusion. *Reasoned judgment* is any belief or conclusion reached on the basis of careful thought and reflection, distinguished from mere or unreasoned opinion on the one hand, and from simple fact on the other.

Distinguishing Between Wants, Needs, and Rights – A *want* is a desire, whereas a *need* is a necessity and *rights* constitute entitlements. *Human rights* are mutual, equal, universal, non-discriminatory, inalienable, indivisible, and interdependent.

Diversity – The representation of multiple groups within a larger group, community, or area, such as a school or a workplace.

Economic Globalization – The continuing integration of markets through global trade by way of trade agreements, such as the North American Free Trade Agreement (NAFTA), trade organizations, such as the World Trade Organization (WTO), and regional economic blocs, such as the European Union (EU). Economic Globalization is the subject of heated debate: Supporters argue that globalization generates wealth, increases trade, and spurs development, while critics argue that globalization leads to environmental degradation, exploitation of the poor by powerful states and companies, and does not support sustainable development.

Economic Justice – Fairness and equity in economic affairs, by establishing laws, governments, and institutions that treat people equally and avoid favoring particular individuals or groups while providing opportunities to those living in poverty.

Economic, Social, and Cultural Rights – Rights that concern the production, development, and management of material for the necessities of life. These rights also include the right to preserve and develop one's cultural identity, as well as rights that give people social and economic security, sometimes referred to as security-oriented rights. Examples of such rights include the rights to adequate education, food, shelter, and health care.

Empathy – The ability to listen deeply to another person's story or experience and connect to the person's feelings and story.

Environmental, Cultural, and Developmental Rights – These rights recognize that people have the right to live in a safe and healthy environment and that groups of people have the right to cultural, political, and economic development.

Environmental Degradation – The diminishment of an ecosystem or a biosphere due to human activity. *Environmental degradation* occurs when natural resources (such as trees, habitat, earth, water, air) are consumed faster than they can be replenished. Sustainability requires that human activity, at a minimum, only uses nature's resources to the point where they can be replenished naturally.

Equality – This human rights principle mandates the same treatment of persons. The notion of fairness and respect for the inherent dignity of all human beings, as specified in Article 1 of the *Universal Declaration of Human Rights*: "All human beings are born free and equal in dignity and rights."

Ethnocentrism – A practice of consciously or unconsciously privileging one's own ethnic group over others that involves judging other groups by the values of one's own group.

Examining Assumptions – Process of deconstructing and analyzing the bases of ideas generally taken for granted in a given society or school of thought. An assumption is something taken for granted or accepted as true without proof, and can be a generalization based on limited or nonexistent experience. Identifying and considering the validity of assumptions are critical thinking skills.

Freedom – Political independence, *liberty*.

Fulfilling Civic and Social Responsibilities – Carrying out the duties associated with *Civic Engagement* – that is, participating in public life, encouraging other people to participate in public life, and joining in common work that promotes the well-being of everyone.

Genocide – A crime defined in international law as acts intended to destroy, in whole or in part, a national, ethnic, racial, or religious group of human beings.

Government – The act or process of governing, especially the decision-making and implementation of public policy in a political unit. The authority, leadership, or agent responsible for promoting and protecting human rights.

Government Responsibility – The obligations that a government must fulfill. Human Rights are an integral

Injustice (Opposite: Justice) – Denying fair, moral, and impartial treatment of the human rights of all persons.

Integrating Human Rights into Personal Awareness and Behaviors – To perceive one's own existence in terms of human rights, including one's own traits, feelings, and behaviors. Self–awareness is a personal understanding of the very core of one's own identity.

Interdependence – Human rights concerns appear in all spheres of life, such as in home, school, workplace, court, and markets. Human rights violations are interconnected; the loss of one right detracts from other rights. Similarly, promotion of human rights in one area supports other human rights.

Intergovernmental Organizations (IGOs) – Organizations sponsored by multiple governments that seek to coordinate their efforts. Some are regional (e.g., the Council of Europe, the African Union), some are strategic alliances (e.g., the North Atlantic Treaty Organization, NATO), and some are global or dedicated to a specific purpose (e.g., the United Nations).

International Bill of Human Rights – The combination of the *Universal Declaration of Human Rights (UDHR)*, the *International Covenant on Civil and Political Rights (ICCPR)* and its Optional Protocol, and the *International Covenant on Economic, Social, and Cultural Rights (ICESCR).*

International Covenant on Civil and Political Rights (ICCPR) – A treaty that was adopted in 1966, and entered into force in 1976. The *ICCPR* establishes that all people have a broad range of civil and political rights. One of the components of the *International Bill of Human Rights.*

International Covenant on Economic, Social and Cultural Rights (ICESCR) – A treaty that was adopted 1966, and entered into force 1976. The *ICESCR* declares that all people have a broad range of economic, social, and cultural rights. One of the components of the *International Bill of Human Rights.*

International Labor Organization (ILO) – Organization established in 1919 as part of the Versailles Peace Treaty to improve working conditions and promote social justice; the *ILO* became a specialized agency of the UN in 1946.

International Law – A set of rules generally regarded and accepted as binding in relations between states and nations. International human rights law is a part of international law designed to protect people against torture, inhuman treatment, arbitrary killings, discrimination, failure to take steps to provide adequate food, shelter, healthcare, and other human rights abuses.

Justice – Fairness, equity, and morality in action or attitude in order to promote and protect human rights and responsibilities. In most societies, people work for justice by organizing through different categories of rights, such as civil, political, economic, social, and cultural.

Kindness – Caring for or showing *empathy* for others.

Knowing Human Rights – To know the past, present, and evolving nature of human rights, as found in the *International Bill of Human Rights* and other human rights standards and norms.

Listening to and Understanding Diverse Perspectives – Exercising the ability to listen, understand, and apply diverse perspectives and stories to one's daily experiences.

Literacy (Opposite: Illiteracy) – The ability to read and write in one or more languages. Literacy can also refer to the ability to understand a set of ideas and terms related to a central concept. For example, human rights literacy is the ability to understand and speak in terms of human rights principles and norms.

Member States – Countries that are members of intergovernmental organizations, such as the United Nations.

Moral Rights and Responsibilities – Rights and obligations based on the general principles of fairness and justice; they are often but not always based on religious beliefs. People sometimes feel they have moral rights even when they do not have legal or human rights in a given situation.

Nationalism – A sense of national consciousness exalting one nation above all others and placing primary emphasis on the promotion of its economic and political interests and culture over those of other nations.

Nonbinding – Term referring to a document, such as a *declaration,* that carries no formal legal obligations. It may, however, carry moral obligations or eventually attain the force of law as *customary international law.*

Non-Discrimination (Opposite: Discrimination) – Non-discrimination is vital to the concept of equality. It ensures that no one is denied the protection of their human rights based on external factors. Such factors include age, birth, color, creed, disability, ethnic origin, familial status, gender, language, marital status, political or other opinion, public assistance, race, religion or belief, sex, or sexual orientation. These categories, however, are only examples; they do not mean that discrimination is allowed on other grounds.

Nongovernmental Organizations (NGOs) – Organizations formed by people outside of government. *NGOs* monitor the proceedings of human rights bodies, such as the United Nations, and are the "watchdogs" of the human rights that fall within their mandate. Some are large and international (e.g., the Red Cross, Amnesty International, and the Girl Scouts), while others may be small and local (e.g., an organization to advocate for people with disabilities in a particular city; a coalition to promote women's rights in one refugee camp). Many NGOs have official consultative status with the UN Economic and Social Council.

Nonviolence (or non-violence) – A set of assumptions about morality, power, and conflict that leads its proponents to reject the use of violence in efforts to attain social or political goals. While often used as a synonym for pacifism, since the mid 20th century the term nonviolence has come to embody a diversity of techniques for waging social conflict without the use of violence, as well as the underlying political and philosophical rationale for the use of these techniques.

Oppression – The systematic exploitation of one societal group by another for its own benefit. The phenomenon involves institutional control, ideological domination, and the imposition of the dominant group's culture on the oppressed.

Passivity – The condition of being inactive or submissive.

Persecution – Violation of the rights of an individual or group by another individual or group. The most common forms are ethnic, racial, and religious persecution. These types of persecution overlap to some degree, as religion is commonly an aspect of culture and ethnic identities are often intertwined with racial identities. The most common persecution scenario is a majority group mistreating a minority group.

Poverty – Condition of being unable to achieve an adequate standard of living. Today, standards of living vary greatly among and within nations. Nonetheless, the effects of poverty remain constant: hunger, homelessness, lack of education, and lack of resources to fulfill basic human needs. For example, one of the main causes of hunger is poverty. Most people who are starving do not have the means to obtain the food that they need..

Prejudice – An attitude, opinion, or feeling formed without adequate prior knowledge, thought, or reason. *Prejudice* can be prejudgment for or against any individual, group, or object. Any individual or group can hold *prejudice(s)* towards another individual, group, or object.

Problem-Solving – Identifying multiple responses to an issue or dilemma and choosing a response which promotes and protects the human rights of all parties.

Protocol – A *treaty* which modifies another *treaty* (e.g., adding additional procedures or substantive provisions).

Racism – An ideology of racial superiority and hierarchy based on discrimination.

Ratification – Process by which a government confirms a state's action in becoming legally bound by a treaty; formal procedure by which a state becomes bound to a *treaty* after acceptance.

Refugee Displacement – *Displacedpersons* have been forced by dangerous circumstances to leave home for a place of safety within their home country. Such circumstances include natural disasters such as droughts or storms, persecution, social unrest, wars, or revolutions. If a person flees to a place within the home country, he or she is called internally displaced. If that person flees to another country, he or she is called a refugee.

Research – Usingmultiple sources to thoroughly study a human rights topic. Such sources can be books, newspapers, magazine or journal articles, or primary human rights documents (e.g., the Universal Declaration of Human Rights).

Reservation –The exceptions that *State Parties* make to a treaty (e.g., provisions that they do not agree to follow). Reservations, however, may not undermine the fundamental objective and purpose of the *treaty*.

Respect – To honor, appreciate, and treat others with dignity.

Respect for self – Treating oneself with care, love, and appreciation, while valuing one's unique and shared characteristics.

Respect for parents and teachers – Treating parents and teachers with care, respect, and appreciation.

Respect for others – Treating others with care, respect, and appreciation.

Responsibility – Obligation, duty, and/or accountability.

Rule of Law – A government must function or operate in support of written laws, which should be adopted through an established procedure. This principle is intended to be a safeguard against unfair judgments or procedures in individual cases. Hence, those who make and enforce the law must respect and uphold the law.

Security – The level of protection or safety by or for an individual, group, or system against threats to human rights, such as arbitrary detention, food deprivation, or unwarranted physical harm.

Self – The total, essential, or particular being of a person; the individual.

Self-Determination – Political independence on the part of a group without control by people outside of that area.

Self-Expression – Sharing one's thoughts, beliefs, feelings, ideas or personality, through verbal or non-verbal means, including dance, essays,. music, painting, photography, poetry, spoken word, sculpture, etc.

of children throughout the world. UNICEF has a variety of programs that address the organization's priority areas of child protection, early childhood, girl's education, HIV/AIDS, and immunization.

United Nations Commission on Human Rights – Body of the United Nations established to draft human rights standards and otherwise address human rights issues.

United Nations Economic and Social Council (ECOSOC) – A UN council of 54 members primarily concerned with population, economic development, human rights, and criminal justice. This high-ranking body receives and issues human rights reports.

United Nations Educational, Scientific, and Cultural Organization (UNESCO) – Body of the Unites Nations established to advance science and learning in the five areas of Education, Natural Sciences, Social and Human Sciences, Culture, and Communication and Information. The mission of the Social and Human Sciences section of UNESCO is to spur advances and innovation that promote the universal principles of justice, freedom, and human dignity.

United Nations General Assembly – One of the principal organs of the UN, consisting of representatives of all member states. The *General Assembly* issues *declarations,* adopts *conventions* on human rights issues, debates relevant issues, and censures states that violate human rights. The actions of the *General Assembly* are governed by the *United Nations Charter*.

United Nations High Commissioner for Refugees (UNHCR) – United Nations agency charged with facilitating international action to address the problems faced by refugees, as well as to promote and protect their human rights. Such rights include the right to seek asylum and the right to return home voluntarily.

United Nations Office of the High Commissioner on Human Rights (OHCHR) – Body of the United Nations established to press the international community and UN *Member States* to honor and uphold human rights treaties, principles, and norms. The OHCHR also speaks on behalf of the victims of human rights violations.

Bibliography

Alderson, J. *Human Rights and the Police.* Strasbourg: Council of Europe, 1984.

Alston, Philip,ed. *The United Nations and Human Rights, A Critical Appraisal.* Oxford, UK: Oxford University Press, 1992.

Amnesty International, Puerto Rican Section. *Our Rights! Series for Children and Youth.* Rio Piedras, Puerto Rico: Amnesty International, Puerto Rican Section, 1993.

Annas, George J. and Michael A. Grodin. *The Nazi Doctors and the Nuremberg Code.* Oxford UK: Oxford University Press, 1992.

Arab Institute for Human Rights, Amnesty International, Tunisian Section. *Human Rights for Children: The U.N. Convention.* Tunisia: ADHOUA, 1992.

Arnot, M. and G. Weiner. *Gender and the Politics of Schooling.* London: Hutchinson and Open University. 1987.

Barker, Dan, *Maybe Right, Maybe Wrong: A Guide for Young Thinkers.* Buffalo, NY: Prometheus Books, 1992.

Bautista, Liberato, ed. *Human Rights: Biblical and Theological Readings.* Manila: Philippines National Council of Churches, 1988.

Bernstein Tarrow, Norma, ed. *Human Rights and Education.* New York: Pergamon Press, vol.3, Pergamon Comparative and International Education Series, 1987.

Brownlie, Ian. *Basic Documents on Human Rights, 3d ed.* Oxford, UK : Oxford University Press, 1993.

Capotorti, Francesco. *Study on the Rights of Persons Belonging to Ethnic, Religious and Linguistic Minorities.* Geneva: United Nations Centre for Human Rights, 1991.

Cassese, Antonio. *Human Rights in a Changing World.* Philadelphia: Temple University Press, 1990.

Catholic Commission for Justice and Peace in Zimbabwe. *The Hit Kit.* Harare: The Catholic Commission for Justice and Peace in Zimbabwe, 1989.

CEDHOSSAI, *Dossier Pédagogique: Comment éduquer aux droits de l'homme et à la paix?* Dakar, Senegal: CEDHOSSAI, 1991.

Center for the Study of Human Rights. *Twenty-four Human Rights Documents.* New York: Center for the Study of Human Rights, Columbia University, 1992.

Centre for Human Rights. *Teaching and Learning about Human Rights: A Manual for Schools of Social Work and the Social Work Profession.* Geneva: United Nations Centre for Human Rights, 1992.

Clark, John. *Democratizing Development, The Role of Voluntary Organizations.* London: Earthscan Publications Ltd, 1991.

Claude, Richard Pierre, and Burns H. Weston, eds. *Human Rights in the World Community: Issues and Action, 2d ed. Philadelphia: University of Pennsylvania Press, 1992.*

Collins, Michael, *Adult Education as Vocation.* London: Routledge, 1991.

Committee for the Protection of Democratic Rights (CPDR), *Know Your Rights: A Handbook for Political Activists, Social Workers, Trade Unionists.* Bombay: Kobad Ghandy (1980)

Council for Cultural Co-operation, *Compendium of Information on Intercultural Education Schemes in Europe: Education of Migrants' Children.* Strasbourg: Council of Europe, 1983.

Daes, Erica-Irene A. *Status of the Individual and Contemporary International Law.* Geneva: United Nations Centre for Human Rights, 1992.

Dembo, David, Clarence J. Dias, Ayesha Kadwani and Ward Morehouse, *Nothing to Lose But Our Lives, Empowerment to Oppose Industrial Hazards in a Transnational World.* New York: new Horizons Press, in cooperation with the Asian Regional Exchange for New Alternatives, Hong Kong and the Indian Law Institute, New Delhi, 1988.

Development Education Centre, *Do It Justice: Resources and Activities for Introducing Education in Human Rights.* Birmingham, UK, 1988.

Dias, Clarence J.,ed. *Initiating Human Rights Education at the Grassroots; Asian Experiences.* Bangkok: Asian Cultural Forum on Development, 1992.

Donnelly, Jack. *International Human Rights.* Boulder, CO: Westview Press, 1993.

Dubé, Ginette and Angela Smailes, eds. *AIDS and Human Rights: Sharing the Challenge.* Vancouver: Vancouver World AIDS Group , 1992.

Eide, Asbørn, and Marek Thee, eds. *Frontiers of Human Rights Education.* Oslo: Universitetsforlaget. 1983.

Eide, Asbørn, et al. *Violations des droits de l'homme: quel recours, quell resistance? = Resistant Against Human Rights Violations.* Paris: Serbal, for UNESCO, 1984.

Finkelstein, Barbara, and Anne E. Imamura and Joseph J. Tobin, eds. *Transcending Stereotypes: Experiencing Culture and Education in Japan.* Yarmouth, MA: Intercultural Press, 1991.

Forsythe, David, *Human Rights and World Politics, 2d ed.* Lincoln, NE: University of Nebraska Press, 1988.

Frankel, Marvin E. with Helen Saideman, *Out of the Shadows of Night: The Struggle for International Human Rights.* New York: Delacorte Press, 1989.

Freire, Paulo. *Pedagogy of the Oppressed.* New York: Seabury Press, 1973.

Fuente, Carmen, and Mercedes Muñoz-Repiso. *Preparation for Life in a Democratic Society in Five Countries in Southern Europe.* Strasbourg: Council of Europe, 1982.

Garcia, Edmundo G. *The Human Rights Reader.* Manila: National Bookstore, 1990.

Gloppen and Lise Rakner. *Human Rights and Development, The Discourse in the Humanities and Social Sciences.* Fantoft-Bergen, Norway: Chr. Michelsen Institute, 1993.

Gordinne, P.,ed. *Droits de l'homme, droits des peuples: guide pour l'information et l'education = Human Rights, Peoples' Rights: Guide for Information and Education.* Brussels: Médiathèque de la Communauté Française de Belgique, 1989.

Graves, Norman J., ed. *Teaching for International Understanding, Peace and Human Rights.* Paris: UNESCO, 1984.

Graves, Norman J.,ed. *Teaching for International Understanding, Peace and Human Rights.* Paris: UNESCO, 1984.

Green, Jennifer, and the Human Rights Program, Harvard Law School. *The Harvard Guide to Human Rights Research.* Cambraidge, MA: 1994.

Gruschow, Janet and Kari Hannibal. *Health Services for the Treatment of Torture and Trauma Survivors.* Washington, DC: American Association for the Advancement of Science, 1989.

Meron, Theodor. *Human Rights and Humanitarian Norms as Customary Law.* Oxford, UK: Oxford University Press, 1991.

New York State Education Department. *Teaching About the Holocaust and Genocide.* Albany, NY: The State Education Department, The Human Rights Series, 1985, 1986.

Newman, Frank, and David Weissbrodt. *International Human Rights.* Cincinnati: Anderson Publishing Co., 1990.

Olguin, Leticia, ed. *Educación y derechos humanos: una discusión interdisciplinaria = Education and Human Rights: An Interdisciplinary Discussion.* San Jose, Costa Rica: Instituto Interamericano de Derechos Humanos, 1989.

Ouane, Adama. *Handbook on Learning Strategies for Post-Literacy and Continuing Education.* Hamburg: UNESCO Institute for Education. 1989.

Ramsey, Patricia. *Teaching and Learning in a Diverse World.* New York: College Press of the Columbia University of the City of New York, 1987.

Randall, Glenn R, and Ellen L. Lutz. *Serving Survivors of Torture.* Washington, DC: American Association for the Advancement of Science, 1991.

Rasmussen, Ole Vedel. *Medical Aspects of Torture.* Copenhagen: Laegeforeningens Forlag, 1990.

Reisman, W. Michael, and Chris T. Antoniou. *The Laws of War: A Comprehensive Collection of Primary Documents on International Laws Governing Armed Conflict.* New York: Vintage Books, 1994.

Reynard, A. *Human Rights in Prisons.* Strasbourg: Council of Europe, 1986.

Richard B. Lillich and Frank C. Newman. *International Human Rights: Problems of Law and Policy.* Boston: Little, Brown and Company, 1979.

Richard Pierre Claude, *Human Rights Education in The Philippines.* Manila: Kalikasan Press, 1991.

Rosenbaum, Alan S., ed. *The Philosophy of Human Rights: International Perspectives.* London: Aldwych Press, 1980.

Secretariado General de la Conferencia Episcopal Peruana, *Rui forastero y me recibieron — La iglesia frente a los hermanos desplazados = I Was a Stranger and They Received Me — The Church and Displaced People.* Lima: Conferencia Episcopal Peruana, 1990.

Selby, David, *Human Rights.* Cambridge, UK: Cambridge University Press, 1988.

Selwood, Sara. *Free Expressions: The Amnesty International Art Education Pack.* London: Amnesty International UK, 1991.

Shiman, David, et al, *Teaching About Human Rights.* Denver: Center for Teaching International Relations, 1988.

Sieghart, Paul. *The International Law of Human Rights.* Oxford, UK: Clarendon Press, 1983.

Smith, Lesley, *Dimensions of Childhood: A Handbook for Social Education at Sixteen Plus.* London: Health Education Authority and UNICEF-UK, 1988.

Spirer, Herbert and Louise. *Data Analysis for Monitoring Human Rights.* Washington, DC: American Association for the Advancement of Science, 1993.

Starkey, Hugh, ed. *Socialization of School Children and Their Education for Democratic Values and Human Rights: Report of the Colloquy of Directions of Educational Research Institutes held in Ericeira, Portugal.* Amsterdam/Lisse: Swets and Zeitlinger, 1991.

Starkey, Hugh, ed. *The Challenge of Human Rights Education.* London: Cassell Education Ltd., for the Council of Europe, 1991.

Stover, Eric and Elena O. Nightingale, M.D. *The Breaking of Bodies and Minds, Torture, Psychiatric Abuse and the Health Professions*. New York: W.H. Freeman and Company, 1985.

Taylor, Charles. *Multiculturalism and the Politics of Recognition*. Princeton, NJ: Princeton University Press, 1992.

Timm, Richard W. *Training of Trainers in Human Rights*. Bangladesh: South Asian Forum for Human Rights (SAFHR), 1992.

Timm, Richard W. *Working for Justice and Human Rights: A Practical Manual*. Dhaka: Hotline Asia Oceania, n.d.

Tomaevski, Katarina. *Women and Human Rights*. London: Zed Books, Ltd., 1993.

Torney-Purta, Judith. *Evaluating Global Education: Sample Instruments for Assessing Programs, Materials and Learning*. New York: Global Perspectives in Education, Inc., 1986-1987.

UNESCO. *Congrès international sur l'enseignement des droits de l'homme = International Congress on the Teaching of Human Rights*. Paris: UNESCO, 1980

UNESCO. *Human Rights Teaching*. Paris: UNESCO, 1986-87.

UNESCO. *World Directory of Human Rights Teaching and Research Institutions*. Paris: Berg Publishers, 1988.

United Nations. *Human Rights: Questions and Answers*. New York: United Nations, 1987.

United Nations. *Symposium on the Role of the Police in the Protection of Human Rights*. New York: United Nations (Doc.No. ST/HR/Ser.A/6), 1980.

University of Botswana. *Human Rights and You*. Gaborone: Macmillan Botswana Publishing, 1989.

Vasak, Karel, ed. and Philip Alston, English Edition, ed. *The*

International Dimensions of Human Rights, 2 vols. Westport, CT: Greenwood Press for UNESCO, 1982.

Vicaría de la Solidaridad. *Religion.* Santiago, Chile: Vicaría de la Solidaridad, Ediciones Paulinas, Manuales de educación en derechos humanos, 1991.

Vincent, R.J. *Human Rights and International Relations.* Cambridge, UK: Cambridge University Press, 1990.

Walker, Jamie. *Violence et résolution des conflits a l'école = Violence and Resolution of Conflicts at School.* Strasbourg: Council of Europe, 1990.

Weiner, G., and M. Arnot. *Gender Under Scrutiny: New Inquiries in Education.* London: Hutchinson and Open University, 1987.

Williams, Roy, *Children and World Development: A Resource Book for Teachers.* London: UNICEF-UK and The Richmond Publishing Co.,Ltd., 1987.

World University Service. *Academic Freedom, A Human Rights Report, vols. 1 and 2. London: Zed Books, Ltd., 1990.*

Zalaquett, Jose. *The Human Rights Issue and the Human Rights Movement.* Geneva: The World Council of Churches, 1981.

Index